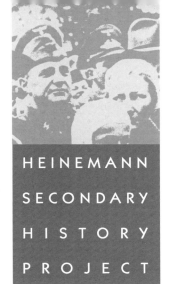

HEINEMANN

SECONDARY

HISTORY

PROJECT

WEIMAR and NAZI GERMANY

FOUNDATION EDITION

Fiona Reynoldson

Heinemann Educational Publishers
Halley Court, Jordan Hill, Oxford OX2 8EJ
A Division of Reed Educational &
Professional Publishing Ltd

OXFORD MELBOURNE AUCKLAND
JOHANNESBURG BLANTYRE GABORONE
IBADAN PORTSMOUTH (NH) USA CHICAGO

© Fiona Reynoldson 1996
The moral rights of the propietor have been asserted.

First published 1996

05 04 03 02
11 10 9 8 7 6

British Library Cataloguing in Publication data
is available from the British Library on request.

ISBN 0 435 30860 2

Produced by Visual Image
Printed by Mateu Cromo in Spain
Cover design by The Wooden Ark Studio

Acknowledgements
The publishers would like to thank the following for
permission to reproduce photographs:

Akadamie der Kunste/Heartfield Archive: 20, 36; AKG
London: 9 top, 11E, 15, 18, 31, 32, 47, 62, 71, 84, 86 bottom;
Bauhaus Archive: 16B; Bildarchiv Preussischer Kulturbesitz:
16A, 17C, 66K; Bilderdienst Suddeutscher Verlag: 4, 5, 14, 26,
35, 40, 43 right, 51, 53D, 60, 70, 73, 80, 86 top; Bridgeman Art
Library/Lauros-Giraudon: 76C; Bridgeman Art
Library/Prado, Madrid: 76D; Bridgeman Art
Library/Vatican Museums and Galleries, Rome: 76E;
Bundesarchiv Koblenz: 13J, 66J; Centre for the Study of
Cartoon and Caricature, University of Kent, David Low/Solo
Syndication: 42D; Lujcan Dodroszycki: 87; Zoe Dominic: 17D;
The Federal Republic of Germany: 57B; The C.L. Hall
Collection: 13I, 23, 25, 45, 46, 58F, 61, 67, 76C, 77E, 77F; Chris
Honeywell: 11D; The Hoover Institution Archives: 21, 34F,
35H; Hulton Getty Collection: 43 left, 62, 92; Imperial War
Museum: 68F, 77D, 81E; Kobal Collection: 59I;
Kunstmuseum/Paul Klee Stiftung, Berne: 56; Pictorial Press:
81G; Popperfoto: cover, 9 bottom, 41B, 42G, 82; Topham
Picture Source: 39, 78; Ullstein Bilderdienst: 7, 13H, 48, 53E,
68, 86 bottom, 93; Weimar Archive: 33, 52; Wiener Library: 34,
44, 50, 54, 59H; Yad Vashem Holocaust Martyrs' and Heroes'
Remembrance Authority: 88C and D.

Details of written sources
In some sources the wording or sentence structure has been
simplified to ensure that the source is accessible.

Richard Bessel (ed.), *Life in the Third Reich*, Oxford University
Press, 1987: 4.2M
M. Berwick, *The Third Reich*, Wayland, 1971: 5.6A, 5.6B
Christabel Bielenberg, *The Past is Myself*, Corgi, 1970: 5.7.1
E. Amy Buller, *Darkness over Germany*, Longman, 1945: 4.3H
H.C. Brandenburg, *Die Geschichte der Hitlerjugend*, Cologne,
1968: 2.6.1
M. Broszat, *The Hitler State*, London, 1981: 5.3B
Karl von Clausewitz, *On War*, Penguin, 1982: 5.1A

The Daily Telegraph, May 1933: 4.6.4
S.C. Dekel and L.M. Lagnado, *Children of the Flames*, London,
1991: 5.3E
Lucjan Dobroszycki (ed.), *The Chonicle of the Lodz*, Ghetto
1941 – 1944, Yale University Press, 1994: 5.4A
Bernt Engelmann, *In Hitler's Germany*, Mandarin,
1989: 4.6.2
Anne Frank, *The Diary of Anne Frank*, Pan Books, 1968: 5.3G
Sara Grober, *Jewish Public Activities in the Lodz Ghetto*,
1979: 5.4B
R. Grunberger, *A Social History of the Third Reich*, Weidenfeld
and Nicolson, 1971: 4.1F, 4.3D, 4.3E, 4.3F
C.W. Guillebaud, *The Economic Recovery of Germany from 1933
to the incorporatioin of Austria in March 1938*, Macmillan,
1939: 4.1A
S. William Halperin, *Germany Tried Democracy*, New York,
1965: 1.5B
S.M. Harrison, *World Conflict in the Twentieth Century*,
Macmillan, 1987:
K. Hildebrand, *The Third Reich*, London, 1984: 5.3A
Adolf Hitler, *Mein Kampf*, (1924 trans. R. Mannheim) Sentry
Paperbacks, 1943: 1.9.1, 2.2G, 3.3A, 3.8.3, 5.1C, 5.1D
Adolf Hitler, *Second Book,* New York, 1962: 2.2H, 5.1E
Illustrated London News, August 1936: 3.8.5
Ian Kershaw, in *History Today*, 198?: 4.5B
A. Klonne, *Youth in the Third Reich*, 1982: 4.2I
H. Krausnick, *The Anatomy of the SS State*, London, 1968: 3.3G
J. Laver (ed.), *Imperial and Weimar Germany*, Hodder and
Stoughton, 1992: 1.8C, 2.2F, 2.4B, 2.4E, 2.4G, 3.5B, 4.2D,
5.5A, 5.5C
G. Le Bon, *The Crowd: A Study of the Popular Mind*, Ernest
Benn, 1952: 2.6.5
R. Leonhard, *A Fairy Tale of Christmas*, (trans. J. Cleugh: 1.8A
W. Maser, *Hitler's Letters and Notes*, Heinemann, 1974: 5.6C
G. Mosse, *Nazi Culture*, W.H. Allen, 1966: 4.2H
J. Noakes, in *History Today*, 1985: 4.4A
J. Noakes and G. Pridham (eds.) *Documents on Nazism
1919 – 1945*, Jonathan Cape, 1974: 2.1B, 2.1C, 2.1D, 2.1F,
2.1G, 2.2C, 2.3A, 2.3B, 2.3D, 2.3E, 3.3J, 3.4B, 3.4H, 3.5G, 3.8,
4.1I, 4.3B, 5.2F, 5.3C, 5.3H, 5.5B, 5.6E
J. Remak, *The Nazi Years*, Prentice-Hall, 1969: 2.2B, 2.2D, 2.4D,
3.2C, 3.2E, 3.3H, 3.3I, 3.4C, 3.4E, 3.5E, 3.5H, 4.5A, 5.1B, 5.2C,
5.3F
Martin Roberts, *Britain and Europe, 1848 – 1980*, Longman,
1986: 5.7.2
Philip Sauvain, *The Era of the Second World War*, Stanley
Thornes, 1993: 5.7.4
William Shirer, *Rise and Fall of the Third Reich*, Pan Books,
1968: 2.6.3
L.L. Snyder, *The Weimar Republic*, Van Nostrand, 1966: 1.2B,
1.2D, 1.3A, 1.5G, 1.6B, 1.6D
Otto Strasser, *Hitler and I*, London, 1940: 2.6.4
Sir J. Wheeler-Bennett, *The Nemesis of Power*, Macmillan, 1953
3.2F
Schools Council General Studies Project, *Nazi Education*,
Longman, 1972: 4.2B
The Times, 4 October 1929: 1.9.2
The United States Strategic Bombing Survey, Overall Report,
Washington, 1945: 5.4H

The publishers have made every effort to trace copyright
holders of material in this book. Any omissions will be
rectified in subsequent printings if notice is given to the
publisher.

CONTENTS

CHAPTER 1

THE BIRTH, STRUGGLE AND DEATH OF THE WEIMAR REPUBLIC 1919–33

1.1 How did the Weimar Republic get its name?

Before 1871

Until 1871 there were many separate states in Germany. The strongest state was Prussia. In 1871, Prussia united all the other states. They became one country called Germany. The capital city of Germany was Berlin which had been in Prussia.

After the First World War

The German people had fought a long war against Britain and France. By 1918, they had lost the war. There was fighting in Berlin. There was chaos everywhere. Early in 1919, a new capital city was chosen. This capital was the beautiful city of Weimar. The new government was named after this city of Weimar.

1.2 How did Germany become a republic?

After the First World War, the German people felt let down. There was a shortage of food. The army and navy were tired of fighting and some soldiers and sailors mutinied. On 9 November the **Kaiser**, or Emperor, abdicated and fled to Holland. Now the Germans had no government. Something had to be done. Germany decided to have an elected government with no kaiser or emperor. This was a **democratic republic**.

▶ The end of Scheidemann's speech proclaiming the republic.

Source A

▲ Scheidemann of the Social Democrats proclaiming Germany a republic, 9 November 1918.

Source B

Stand united and loyal and be aware of your duty. The old and rotten – the monarchy has broken down. Long live the new! Long live the German Republic!

The Social Democrats

The Social Democrats were the largest political party in Germany. One of their leaders was Philipp Scheidemann. He said that Germany was now a democratic republic (see Sources A and B).

The Spartacists (Communists)

Some other people wanted Germany to become a Communist country. These people were called Spartacists. They were led by Rosa Luxemburg and Karl Liebknecht (see Sources C and D).

The Spartacist uprising

In January 1919 the Spartacists tried to seize power in Berlin. The Social Democrats were afraid of the Spartacists and of Communism. They joined with the army to put down the Spartacist uprising. Thousands of Spartacists were killed and their leaders, Rosa Luxemburg and Karl Liebknecht were both shot in cold blood. The Communists never forgot this. They saw the Social Democrats as their deadly enemies.

ROSA LUXEMBURG (1871–1919)

Rosa Luxemburg was born in Poland but became a German citizen when she married. She was imprisoned in 1915 for speaking out against the First World War. Later she helped to found the Spartacus League (the Spartacists). This became the German Communist Party (KPD).

She was nicknamed 'Red Rosa' and was a good speaker and writer. She was killed by the army during the Berlin uprising in January 1919.

QUESTIONS

1 Look at page 4. Germany lost the First World War. What was the effect of this on the German people?

2 Read **The Spartacists** and **the Spartacist uprising**.

   a Who were the Spartacists?
   b Write a few sentences about the events of January 1919.

Source C

▲ A Spartacist meeting in Berlin, 30 December 1918.

Source D

MEN AND WOMEN OF LABOUR! COMRADES!

The [communist] revolution has come to Germany. The soldiers, who for four years were driven to the slaughterhouse to fill rich men's pockets, have revolted. The workers, who for four years were exploited and starved, have revolted. The Kaiser has fled. Workers' and Soldiers' Councils have been formed everywhere. We call to you: Arise for action!'

▲ From the *Spartacist Manifesto*, 29 November 1918.

Source A

From the **constitution** of the Weimar Republic. The constitution is the set of laws that explains how the country is run.

Article 1: The German Reich is a Republic. Power comes from the people.

Article 22: The members of the Reichstag are elected by men and women over 20 years of age.

Article 48: In an emergency the President may take control and use the army to restore order.

Article 54: The Chancellor and government must have the support of the Reichstag [parliament].

▲ Articles from the Constitution of the Weimar Republic.

The way the Weimar Republic was run is shown at the bottom of the page.

Strengths of the Weimar Republic

In some ways the laws of the Weimar Republic were very democratic. Men and women had the vote at the age of 20. (In Britain the age for men was 21 and for some women 30.) The head of the government (the **Chancellor**) had to have the support of most of the people in the **Reichstag** or parliament. Voting was by **proportional representation**. This meant that the number of seats each party had in the Reichstag was based on the number of votes they got. For example, if a party won ten per cent of the votes it was given ten per cent of the seats.

Weaknesses of the Weimar Republic

There were also laws which could weaken democracy. In an emergency (or crisis) the head of state (the **President**) could sack the Chancellor, ignore the Reichstag and rule by his own laws. This was allowed under **Article 48** of the Constitution (see Source A).

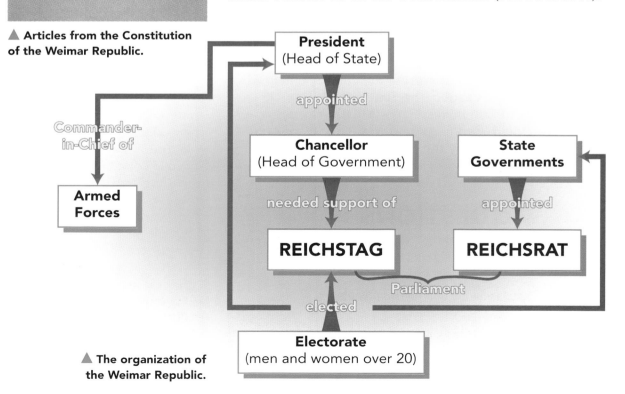

▲ The organization of the Weimar Republic.

Problems

Difficult to make decisions. The system of proportional representation (see page 6) in the Reichstag meant that no one party had a majority. This was because so many parties were able to win seats in the Reichstag. They often could not agree and this made it difficult for the government to make decisions. If there was a lot of disagreement, it was tempting for the President to suspend democracy and rule by his own laws. This happened a lot after 1930.

Some groups disliked democracy. There were several groups who were against democracy. They were very traditional and right-wing. One of these was the **army** led by such men as Hindenburg and Ludendorff. Another group was the **civil service** which did not like change. The third group were the **lawyers** and **judges** which were sympathetic to the right-wing. None of them liked the new democractic Weimar Republic.

How did this affect the Weimar Republic?

The Weimar Republic had to work with the army, the civil service and the judges in the day to day running of Germany. This made governing difficult for the new democratic Weimar Republic.

Source C

▲ A cartoon showing how judges did not want to be hard on right wing demonstrators.

QUESTIONS

1 Read page 6.
   a List the laws which made the Weimar Republic a strong democracy.
   b Which law could weaken democracy?

2 Read page 7.
   a Why was it often difficult for the government to rule?
   b Which groups did not like democracy?
   c What effect did this have?

Source B

◀ The new army (Reichswehr) was led by the men who had fought in the First World War. On the left is Ludendorff. They are wearing the old style uniforms.

Look at the chart on the right. As you will see, there were many different political parties.

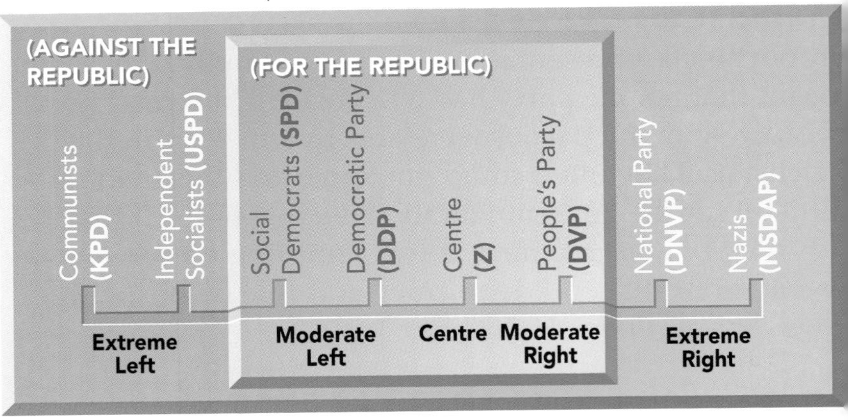

Left-wing parties

1 The Spartacists became the German Communist Party (or KPD). The Communists hated the Weimar Republic because it had put down the Spartacist uprising in 1919.

2 The Independent Socialists (USPD). wanted a communist government like the one in Bolshevik Russia. This party joined up with the Communists.

Moderate parties

1 The Social Democratic Party (SPD) set up the Republic. Its leaders became the first President and Chancellor. They wanted democracy. They disliked Communism.

(AGAINST THE REPUBLIC)		(FOR THE REPUBLIC)					
Communists (KPD)	Independent Socialists (USPD)	Social Democrats (SPD)	Democratic Party (DDP)	Centre (Z)	People's Party (DVP)	National Party (DNVP)	Nazis (NSDAP)
Extreme Left		Moderate Left		Centre	Moderate Right		Extreme Right

▲ The parties of the Weimar Republic, ranging from left-wing to right-wing. (They are given English names but German initials.)

2 The Democratic Party (DDP) was made up of lawyers and intellectuals.

3 The Centre Party (Z) did not like either the extreme right or the extreme left.

4 The People's Party (DVP) was very patriotic but supported the Weimar Republic.

Right-wing parties

1 The National Party (DNVP) did not like democracy. It wanted the government to be strong. This was the way to make Germany a great military power again.

2 The German Workers' Party (DAP) soon became the National Socialist German Workers' Party (NSDAP). Later this became known as the Nazi Party.

		Jan 1919	June 1920	May 1924	Dec 1924	May 1928	Sept 1930	July 1932	Nov 1932
	Nazis	**(NSDAP)**	–	–	32	14	12	107	230	196
	National Party	**(DNVP)**	44	71	95	103	73	41	37	52
	People's Party	**(DVP)**	19	65	45	51	45	30	7	11
	Centre	**(Z)**	91	64	65	69	62	68	75	70
	Democratic Party	**(DDP)**	75	39	28	32	25	20	4	2
	Social Democrats	**(SPD)**	165	102	100	131	153	143	133	121
	Independent Socialists	**(USPD)**	22	84	–	–	–	–	–	–
	Communists	**(KPD)**	–	4	62	45	54	77	89	100

(Left margin labels: AGAINST THE REPUBLIC / FOR THE REPUBLIC)

▲ The results of national elections to the Reichstag, 1919–32.

DATE	PARTY OF CHANCELLOR	CHANCELLOR	PRESIDENT
1919	SPD	Scheidemann	Ebert (SPD)
1919–20	SPD	Bauer	
1920	SPD	Müller	
1920–1	Z	Fehrenbach	
1921–2	Z	Wirth	
1922–3	Non-party	Cuno	
1923	DVP	Stresemann	
1923–5	Z	Marx	
1925–6	Non-party	Luther	
1926–8	Z	Marx	Hindenburg (Non-party)
1928–30	SPD	Müller	
1930–2	Z	Brüning	
1932	Non-party	Papen	
1932	Non-party	Schleicher	
1933	Nazi	Hitler	

◀ The governments of the Republic 1919–33, showing the parties involved, the Chancellors and the Presidents.

Who supported the parties?

This is difficult to tell because all the voting was by secret ballot.

The working classes It seems likely that the working classes supported the parties of the left – the SPD (Social Democrats) or the KPD (Communists).

The middle classes The way the middle classes voted varied a great deal. Many liked the moderate, thoughtful DDP (Democratic Party). Others wanted Germany to be great and powerful again. They liked the DVP (People's Party). The Centre Party (Z) put religion first. It was supported by those people who thought religion was very important.

Wealthy business men often supported the right wing DNVP (National Party).

Later many middle class people voted for the Nazi Party because they thought it offered the best hope of jobs and of making Germany rich and powerful once more.

QUESTIONS

1 Look at the diagram at the top of page 8. Which parties
   a supported and
   b opposed the Weimar Republic?

2 Look at the chart at the bottom of page 8. Write out the following sentences filling in the gaps.

   In the elections of 1919 the _____ won the most votes. The KPD and the _____ won no votes at all.

   By May 1924 the _____ had disappeared as a separate party.

   The best year for the SPD was _____ when they won _____ seats. After that they slowly lost popularity.

   All the time the KPD were gaining seats. By November 1932 they had _____ seats in the Reichstag. This was not as many as the SPD with _____ seats.

   However, far in front, by 1932, was the _____ party with _____ seats.

3 Look at the chart at the top of page 9.

   a How many times did the government change between 1919 and 1933?
   b Why was this the case? (Look back to page 7.)

What is a crisis?

A crisis in a disease is the point when a patient is balanced between recovery and dying. The Weimar Republic had two crises. The first crisis was between 1919 and 1923. The republic recovered. The second crisis was between 1929 and 1933. The republic died.

The three causes of the crisis of 1919·–1923 were:
1 The treatment of Germany by the Allies.
2 Economic difficulties (to do with money).
3 Political difficulties (uprisings against the government).

Germany and the Treaty of Versailles

Germany surrendered to the Allies on 11 November 1918. In June 1919 Germany signed the Treaty of Versailles. It said that Germany had caused the war and Germany was responsible for all the war damage.

Land taken away from Germany

Look at the map below. It shows the land that was taken

Source A

Germany accepts that she and her allies are to blame for causing all the losses and damage...as a result of the War.

▲ Taken from Article 231 (the War Guilt clause) in the Treaty of Versailles.

Source B

Giving in to the might of the Allies, the government of the German Republic accepts the peace treaty. But the government of the German Republic is still convinced that the peace treaty is unfair.

▲ Adapted from an official statement made by the German Government in June 1919.

► Land lost by Germany by the Treaty of Versailles in 1919.

...way from Germany and given to France, Denmark, Belgium and Poland. Also Germany's colonies in places like Africa were taken away and given mainly to France and Britain to look after.

A small army and navy
Germany was only allowed an army of 100,000 soldiers and a navy of six battleships. No airforce was allowed. The Rhineland was **demilitarized** (see map).

Reparations (paying back the costs of the war)
In 1921 the Allies told Germany to pay £6,600 million to the Allies for all the damage done. Already some railway stock and other machines had been taken in to pay for the war damage.

Inflation
Inflation is when prices go up and up. This happened in Germany in 1921. The news of the **reparations** bill was one reason. German businessmen speculating to make money was another.

Source C

Vengeance! German nation! Today the disgraceful treaty is being signed. Do not forget it. The German people will press forward to reconquer the place among nations to which it is entitled. Then will come vengeance for the shame of 1919.

▲ From *Deutsche Zeitung*, a German newspaper, 28 June 1919.

Source D

▲ Original German bank notes from 1921 and 1923. They are for millions of marks.

Source E

◀ German children playing with bundles of bank notes made worthless by the inflation, 1923.

In 1923, the French invaded the Ruhr, part of the Rhineland, to collect reparations Germany owed them. This was the last straw. The German currency (money) collapsed because the German people had no confidence in it. Money was worthless (see Source E). Many people lost all their savings.

How the German people felt

At first the Germans were angry with the Allies. Then they were angry with their own Government (the Weimar Republic) which had agreed to the Treaty of Versailles.

The danger to the German Government

The Government printed masses of paper money. People took wheelbarrows to work to collect their wages. But their wages were worth less and less as prices went up and up. This made ordinary German people very discontented. Many of them started to listen to men and women who wanted to overthrow the Government. There were two right-wing uprisings against the Weimar Republic.

1 The Kapp *Putsch* (revolt) 1920. Dr Wolfgang Kapp marched on Berlin with 5,000 supporters (see Source H). He wanted to set up a right-wing government. However, the Government called for a general strike of gas, water, electricity and transport workers to stop Kapp taking control. He fled abroad.

2 The Munich *Putsch* 1923. Adolf Hitler was the new leader of the Nazi Party. He and General Ludendorff tried to lead a march from Munich to Berlin to overthrow the Government. The march was broken up by the police and Hitler was arrested.

Similarities and differences

The leaders of the two uprisings blamed the German Government for the surrender of Germany in 1918. Both Kapp and Hitler accused the German Government of stabbing the German army in the back. They said that the German army had not lost the war but were betrayed by the Weimar politicians. And the German

Source F

1918
0.63 marks

1922
163 marks

Jan. 1923
250 marks

July 1923
3,465 marks

Sept. 1923
1,512,000 marks

Nov. 1923
201,000,000,000 marks

▲ The rising cost of a loaf of bread in Berlin.

Source G

As soon as I received my salary I rushed out to buy food. My daily pay as an editor was just enough to buy one loaf of bread and a small piece of cheese or some oatmeal. A clergyman friend came to Berlin with his monthly salary to buy a pair of shoes for his baby; he could buy only a cup of coffee.

▲ Dr Frieda Wunderlich, a journalist, describes the effects of inflation, 1923.

Source H

▲ The flag of the old Second Reich being raised in Berlin during the Kapp *Putsch*, March 1920.

Source I

▲ The swastika flag of the Nazi Party being shown during the Munich *Putsch*, 1923.

Source J

▶ A poster accusing the German Government of 'stabbing the army in the back' in 1918.

people were betrayed again when the Government signed the terrible Treaty of Versailles.

However, Kapp wanted to go back to the great days of old Germany (the Second Reich). Whereas Hitler wanted a new, strong Germany called the **Third Reich** (see glossary on page 94).

QUESTIONS

1 Read the text on pages 10–11. What did the Treaty of Versailles say about
   a who caused the war
   b land
   c Germany's army and navy
   d reparations?

2 Read Sources B and C on pages 10–11. What did the German people feel about the Treaty?

3 Read **Inflation** and **The danger to the German Government**. Why did inflation make the German people even more angry?

4 Read **Similarities and differences**. In what ways were the Kapp *Putsch* and the Munich *Putsch*
   a similar and
   b different?

The Weimar Republic recovered from the crisis of 1923. The next six years turned out to be good ones for Germany.

Source A

▲ A German factory under full production in 1925.

Low inflation

Gustav Streseman became Chancellor and the Government set to work to get inflation under control. All the old paper notes were called in and destroyed. A new currency was started. It was called the **Rentenmark**.

The Dawes Plan 1924

This was an agreement between Germany, the USA, Britain and France. It spread out the paying of the reparations so that Germany only paid when she was able to. The deadline was extended by 58 years.

The recovery of Germany

The Dawes Plan helped Germany. Instead of paying so much money in reparations there was spare money to invest in new factories. Now that Germany was more stable the USA invested money in Germany. Suddenly Germany was leaping ahead. Economic growth was much faster in Germany than it was in Britain or France.

Source B

In many ways the League follows on from the Treaty of Versailles of 1919. This Treaty has caused problems between the League and Germany. I hope that our co-operation within the League will make it easier to discuss these problems. Trust and confidence will be a better creative force than anything else.

▲ Adapted from part of Gustav Stresemann's speech on Germany's entry into the League of Nations in 1926.

Germany and the rest of the world

Stresemann believed that Germany could become great again by co-operating with the other great nations. There was nothing to be gained by looking for revenge. Some people in Germany criticised Stresemann. But he was a very patient man. Although he disliked the Treaty of Versailles and the loss of German land, he was prepared to wait. He believed that once Germany was trusted by the other nations like France and Britain, then the Treaty of Versailles could later be dropped.

The Locarno Pact 1925

In 1925 Stresemann led Germany in the signing of the Locarno Pact with France, Belgium, Britain and Italy. France, Germany and Belgium agreed not to attack each other or change their borders.

The League of Nations

In 1926 Stresemann led Germany into the League of Nations. This organization was formed after the First World War to maintain world peace. Now Germany was part of the international world again. In 1928 Stresemann joined 60 other countries in signing the Kellogg-Briand Pact. They all agreed not to go to war against each other.

The Weimar Republic gets stronger

From 1923 to 1929 the Weimar Republic was much stronger than it had been just after the war. Led by Stresemann in the Reichstag the different parties managed to work together. The extreme parties such as the Nazis gained fewer seats in the elections. The German people were better off and more contented. The Weimar Republic looked safe.

Source C

▲ Three of the statesmen who negotiated the signing of the Locarno Pact in 1925. From left to right: Stresemann, Austen Chamberlain of Britain and Aristide Briand of France.

Source D

I see the importance of this peace between ourselves and France. A nation must not be like a child that writes a list on Christmas Eve of everything it could possibly want for the next fifteen years. The parents could not give the child all it wants. In foreign politics I often feel that I am being given such a list.

▲ Adapted from a speech by Stresemann in 1925. He was defending his signing of the Locarno Pact against critics in Germany.

GUSTAV STRESEMANN (1878–1929)

After the First World War Stresemann became leader of the German People's Party (DVP). From 1921, he believed that all the parties should work together so that Germany would not collapse. He became Chancellor in August 1923. He then became Foreign Minister between November 1923 and 1929.

In all that time he worked to keep the democratic German Government going. He also worked to make Germany trusted again by the other European countries. Then eventually they would be prepared to drop the Versailles Treaty. That was his aim. It was a tragedy that Stresemann died when he did in 1929.

The 1920s was a time of experiment in Germany. As things settled down, writers, musicians and artists tried out new ideas.

Artists

George Grosz was a painter who used art to look at the way people lived. His painting, *Grey Day* (Source A) showed how boring most people's lives were. Architecture and design were affected by the work of **Walter Gropius** and the **Bauhaus** movement (Sources B and C).

Plays and operas

Germany also became the centre for new plays and operas. The most famous playwright was **Bertolt Brecht**. He wrote the *Three-penny Opera* and *The Caucasian Chalk Circle*.

Cinema

This was the time of great advances in films. One film, the *Cabinet of Dr Calgari*, was supposed to be a horror film. In fact, its underlying message was anti-war and anti-military.

Writers

The leading writers were Arnold Zweig, Hermann Hesse, Stefan George, Thomas Mann and **Erich Remarque**. Remarque wrote a moving anti-war novel called *All Quiet on the Western Front*. This described the horrors of the First World War, and within three months it was turned into a highly successful film.

Source A

◀ *Grey Day* by George Grosz, a comment on everyday life in Germany.

Source B

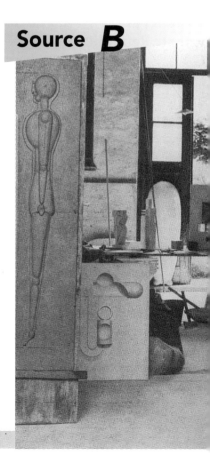

▶ A room in Walter Gropius' house showing the new Bauhaus style of furniture.

Dislike of the new ways

1 People on the right wing did not like the new, free ways of looking at things. The Nazis and the DNVP wanted more traditional patriotic German music and art.

2 People on the left wing such as the Communists felt that the new ways did not reflect the real needs of working people.

3 Many ordinary people liked ordinary pictures, ordinary music and ordinary plays. They could not understand modern music and they did not know what to make of Gropius' furniture.

4 Some people thought moral standards were lower. Berlin had a huge number of nightclubs, even more than Paris.

Art, the Weimar Republic and the Nazis

Cultural life was all very exciting in the 1920s. Germany, and particularly Berlin, was the centre of the new thinking. Germany was again an influence in Europe. But later the Nazis attacked the art of the Weimar Republic. They said it was un-German and immoral.

Source C

▲ The Einstein Tower near Berlin. This was designed by Erich Mendelsohn and shows the new style of architecture – now recognized as 'Thirties'.

Source D

▲ A scene from the *Three-penny Opera* written by Bertolt Brecht in 1928.

WALTER GROPIUS (1883–1969)

Gropius studied architecture and became a leader in design in the 1920s. He developed new buildings and furniture using bold designs and unusual materials. It was called Bauhaus.

When Hitler and the Nazis came to power he had to leave Germany and eventually settled in the United States. He became an American citizen and professor of architecture at Harvard University.

QUESTIONS

1 Read page 16. What new ideas in art, architecture and books came out in the 1920s?

2 Read page 17. What did the Nazis think about the new ideas?

In 1929 there was another crisis in the Weimar Republic. This was started by an economic crisis which then led to a political crisis.

Economic crisis in the USA

The USA lent money to Germany from 1924 onwards. This worked well. The money meant that Germany could rebuild factories and businesses. Both the American and the German economies grew. However, in 1929 disaster struck. The New York stock exchange or money market on Wall Street collapsed. This became known as the **Wall Street Crash**. People lost a lot of money. The USA demanded back all the money it had lent to Germany.

Economic crisis in Germany

Germany was unable to pay the money back. Thousands of businesses collapsed because they had no money to keep them going.

To make it worse other countries like Britain and France were affected by the crisis in the USA. This meant they did not have any money to buy goods from Germany. More businesses collapsed and millions of people were unemployed. Many lost their homes and lived on the streets (see Sources A and B).

Year	Numbers unemployed
1928	1.8
1929	2.9
1930	3.2
1931	4.9
1932	6.0

▲ Unemployment in Germany 1928–32 (in millions).

Source A

No one knew how many there were of them. They sat or lay on the pavements or in the roadway and gravely shared out scraps of newspapers among themselves.

▲ Description, in a short story, of the suffering in Germany caused by the depression.

Source B

► Unemployed people in Hanover queue to receive their dole money, 1932.

Political crisis

It was one thing to keep all the political parties working together when times were good. It was different when times were bad.

The leader of the SPD refused to agree to cut unemployment benefit. The Centre Party said the benefit must be cut. The two parties split and this left the Centre Party trying to govern without a majority in the Reichstag.

The slide to dictatorship

Without a majority in the Reichstag the leader of the Centre Party had to ask the President to use his emergency powers. This meant that laws could be made without having to go through the Reichstag. The President was **Paul von Hindenburg**. He did not like democracy and he was happy to keep using his emergency powers. So between 1930 and 1932 the Reichstag sat less often and became more and more helpless.

The events of 1932–33

Hindenburg supported two new leaders who wanted to end democracy, but since they were bitter enemies they soon fell out. They were called **Franz von Papen** and **Kurt von Schleicher**.

Papen persuaded Hindenburg to get rid of his rival. Then persuaded him to appoint a completely new Chancellor. The new Chancellor was **Adolf Hitler**, the leader of the **Nazi Party**.

Both Papen and Hindenburg thought that they could easily control this new Chancellor. They could not have been more wrong.

Year	Decrees issued
1930	5
1931	44
1932	60

▲ The number of decrees (laws) issued under the emergency powers, 1930–32.

Year	Times Reichstag sat
1930	94
1931	41
1932	13

▲ The number of sittings of the Reichstag, 1930–32.

Source C

The one good thing could be that the National Socialists [Nazis] have passed their peak... but against this stands the fact that extreme policies of the right have sparked off a strong reaction on the left. The Communists have made gains almost everywhere.

▲ Adapted from part of a memorandum about the Reichstag election of July 1932.

Why did democracy collapse in the Weimar Republic?

The Republic had problems from the beginning:

1 Many people held on to the old ideas and ways of thinking and were against democracy..
2 It was attacked from the left by Communists and the right by Nazis.
3 Outside pressures (Germany was forced to give up land and to pay reparations).
4 Economic problems (not enough money to build up businesses and create jobs).

Stresemann kept all the parties working together in the Reichstag so the attacks from the left and right were fended off. He developed good relations with France and Britain. He was able to get the USA to lend Germany money. This helped the economic problems. Stresemann died on 3 October 1929.

Economic and political crisis 1929–33

Shortly after Stresemann's death the Wall Street Crash happened. This caused the collapse of Germany's economy and arguments broke out in the Reichstag about what to do to save Germany. The parties fell out. This allowed the President to use the emergency powers over and over again. In this way democracy was destroyed in Germany.

Source D

DEUTSCHE NATURGESCHICHTE

METAMORPHOSE

▲ A collage by the German artist, John Heartfield, showing what happened to the Weimar Republic. President Ebert is the caterpillar, President Hindenburg the chrysalis (see page 9), and Hitler the butterfly. (A chrysalis is the middle stage in the life cycle of a butterfly.)

QUESTIONS

1 Look at the unemployment figures on page 18. Look at Sources A and B.
   a How many people were unemployed in 1928?
   b How many people were unemployed in 1932?
   c What is the link between the unemployment figures and Sources A and B?

2 Look at the two charts on page 19.
   a When was the Reichstag more powerful – in 1930 or 1932?
   b Explain the connection between the two charts.

Dictatorship

A dictatorship is when a country is ruled by one person. When Adolf Hitler became Chancellor in January 1933, he set out to make Germany a **totalitarian dictatorship**. This means he wanted to have total control of Germany and the lives of the German people.

A PRESIDENT AND THREE CHANCELLORS

The President: Paul von Hindenburg (1847–1934)

Hindenburg had a military career and retired in 1911 at the age of 64. He was recalled to command the German armies in the First World War, together with Ludendorff. The German Government was blamed for losing the war. Many people believed the Government had surrendered and stabbed the army in the back. They believed the army could have gone on fighting. Hindenburg therefore became popular in the 1920s.

He was elected President in 1925. He did not think much of democracy and allowed Germany to slide towards a dictatorship after 1930. He died in 1934 and Hitler took his place as President.

Chancellor 1: Heinrich Brüning (1885–1970)

Brüning was leader of the Centre Party from 1929. With the economic collapse of Germany he found it difficult to get the support of the Reichstag. Instead he ruled by decree. When Hitler came to power, he left Germany.

Chancellor 2: Franz von Papen (1879–1969)

Papen had been a diplomat. He became right wing and did not support democracy. He did a deal with Hitler to keep his rival, Schleicher, out of government in 1933.

Chancellor 3: Kurt von Schleicher (1882–1934)

Schleicher had a military career. He hated democracy but also disliked von Papen and would not work with him. Hitler had him killed in 1934.

Source E

einen·Beſſern findſt·du·nicht·

▲ A poster of Paul von Hindenburg, President of Germany, 1925–34.

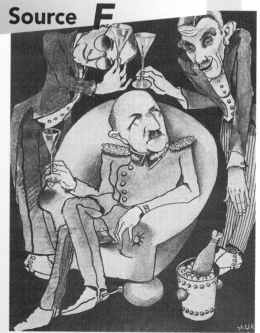

Source F

▲ A cartoon showing the last three chancellors of the Weimar Republic: Brüning (left), Schleicher (centre) and Papen (right).

SUMMARY

- ▶ **1918** Military and naval mutinies. Scheidemann proclaimed Germany a Republic. Germany surrendered to the Allies.
- ▶ **1919** Spartacist uprising in Berlin. Treaty of Versailles.
- ▶ **1920** Kapp *Putsch*.
- ▶ **1921** Amount of reparations announced.
- ▶ **1923** French occupation of the Ruhr. Munich *Putsch*.
- ▶ **1924** Dawes Plan.
- ▶ **1925** Hindenburg elected President. Locarno Pact.
- ▶ **1926** Germany allowed to join the League of Nations.
- ▶ **1928** Kellogg-Briand Pact.
- ▶ **1929** Death of Stresemann. Wall Street Crash.
- ▶ **1930–1** Emergency powers used.
- ▶ **1933** Hitler appointed Chancellor (January).

1.9   Exercise: The Weimar Republic 1919–33

Source *1*

So the war had all been in vain. In vain all the sacrifices. In vain the death of two million soldiers. Had they died for this, so that the wretched criminals of the Weimar Republic could lay hands on the fatherland [Germany]?

▲ Hitler, writing in *Mein Kampf*, about Germany's First World War surrender in November 1918. Hitler wrote *Mein Kampf* ('My Struggle') when he was in prison, following the failure of the Munich *Putsch* of 1923. It told the story of his life so far and explained his ideas. It was first published in 1925.

Source *2*

By the death of Herr Stresemann, Germany has lost her ablest politician. Stresemann worked for the rebuilding of his shattered country. When he became Chancellor, Germany was in ruins. The French were in the Ruhr and the problem of reparations hung over a bankrupt Germany which was full of unrest. Germany is now orderly and prosperous and has a good reputation in Europe.

▲ An obituary of Stresemann which appeared in the British newspaper *The Times*, 4 October 1929. Stresemann died on 3 October 1929.

1 Read **Similarities and differences** on pages 12–13 and Source 1. In Source 1, Hitler says the leaders of the Weimar Republic were 'wretched criminals'. What did Hitler say they had done wrong?

2 a List the four problems the Weimar Republic faced. (See top of page 20.)
  b Write a paragraph saying what Stresemann did to deal with these problems. (See middle of page 20.)

3 Some people say that Stresemann's death in 1929 was a tragedy for Germany. Read **Economic and Political crisis 1929–33** and **Dictatorship** on page 20. Do you think Stresemann would have been able to stop Germany becoming a dictatorship? Explain your answer.

CHAPTER 2

THE RISE OF HITLER TO 1933

Hitler was appointed Chancellor by President Hindenburg in January 1933. How had he reached this position of power? And how had the Nazi party grown so quickly to become the largest party in the Reichstag?

2.1 How did Hitler come to dominate the Nazi Party?

Source A

The beer cellar in Munich where the first meetings of the Nazi Party were held.

Source B

Our little committee, which with its seven members was really the whole party, was nothing but the managing committee of a small card club. To start with, we met in a pathetic little room in a small pub. We discussed letters that we received and wrote the replies.

Hitler's description of the meetings of the German Workers' Party (DAP) in 1919.

Bavaria 1918–23

Like all the states within Germany, Bavaria had its own government. At the end of 1918 the Bavarians had a communist government. However, this was quickly put down and a government loyal to the Weimar Republic was set up. This did not last. In 1920 a right-wing group seized power and set up a new government in the capital city, Munich.

How did this affect the Nazi Party?

The Nazi Party started in Bavaria. From 1920, it was greatly encouraged by the right-wing government in Munich which was led by **Gustav Kahr**. The Nazi Party quickly gained more and more support from people who did not like the Weimar Republic.

The German Workers' Party (DAP)

This was founded in Munich, Bavaria, in 1919 by **Anton Drexler**. Adolf Hitler joined the DAP in September 1919.

The DAP was just one of many small racialist parties in Bavaria at the time. Drexler was a railway mechanic and Hitler was a wounded ex-soldier who hated the Weimar Republic. He felt it had betrayed the German army and lost the war.

Source C

The new movement [Nazi Party] set out to be a racialist movement with a firm social base, and a hold over the broad masses. It was to be welded together in an iron hard organization, and filled with blind obedience.

▲ **From a memorandum by Hitler, 1922.**

Hitler's talents

Hitler was brilliant at speaking to crowds. In the early days of radio and with no television this was very important.

He was also responsible for persuading the party to buy a newspaper (the *Munich Observer*) for putting forward the DAP's views.

He also changed the name of the DAP. It became the National Socialist German Workers' Party or **NSDAP** (this was shortened to **Nazi Party**).

Hitler becomes leader 1921

Hitler became the party leader in 1921. He wanted to build a massive party. Already his magnetic speaking powers made people in the party think of him as the **Führer** – their leader. He wanted his followers to give him their absolute obedience. He wanted to seize power.

Source D

He was holding the masses and me with them, under an hypnotic spell by the sheer force of his own conviction...I forgot everything but the man; then glancing around, I saw that his magnetism was holding these thousands as one.

▲ **Kurt Ludecke listening to Hitler speaking in 1922.**

Hitler and the SA

Hitler needed soldiers if he was to seize power. He set up armed groups within the Nazi Party.

By October 1921 he combined these groups under the name of **Sturm Abteilung (SA)** or Storm troopers.

Why men joined the SA

Many men had fought in the First World War. When Germany surrendered they felt betrayed, just as Hitler had felt. Joining the SA gave these ex-soldiers a purpose in life again.

They loved the brown uniform and the swastika banners. They swore loyalty to Hitler (see Source F). They organized massive parades. Many enjoyed their job of breaking up Communist and Social Democrat meetings – often with violence.

The Munich *Putsch* 1923

With the SA behind him, Hitler tried to take over the Bavarian government. In November 1923 he burst into a meeting where **Gustav von Kahr**, the head of the Bavarian government was speaking. Hitler brandished a revolver and said he was taking over the Bavarian government.

▲ **The SA displaying the swastika. The words on the flag say, 'Germany awake'.**

Then he said he would march on Berlin and take over the German government. He tried to persuade Kahr to join him.

Kahr refuses to join Hitler

Kahr refused to join Hitler and escaped from a locked room in the night.

The next day armed police called out by Kahr broke up a march of Hitler's supporters and the SA. Sixteen of the marchers were killed. Hitler was caught and put on trial for treason.

Source **F**

As a member of the storm troop of the NSDAP, I pledge myself by its storm flag: to be always ready to stake life and limb in the struggle for the aims of the movement; to give absolute military obedience to my leaders.

▲ **Part of the pledge taken by members of the SA.**

Hitler on trial

Hitler had hoped that Kahr would join him. (Kahr did not like the Weimar Republic either). However, Kahr did not like the idea and the army did not support Hitler. Hitler had failed. But he was so persuasive that he turned his trial into an attack on the Republic. He convinced many people that he was a patriotic man, doing his best for Germany.

Hitler sent to prison

Hitler could have been executed. But many people (including the judges) were sympathetic. Hitler was sent to prison for just five years. In the end he only stayed there for nine months.

He spent the time sorting out his ideas and seeing as many visitors as he wished. While he was in prison he wrote a book called *Mein Kampf* ('My Struggle'). In this book he told his life story so far and described his ideas.

Source G

We wanted to create in Germany the situation which alone will make it possible for the iron grip of our enemies to be removed from us... we wanted to create order in the state... and above all, for the highest honourable duty which we, as Germans, know should be once more introduced – the duty of bearing arms, military service. And now I ask you: Is what we wanted high treason?

▲ Hitler's defence at his trial in Munich in 1924.

Source H

▲ A painting, produced in 1933, after Hitler came to power, of Hitler preparing for the Munich *Putsch*.

QUESTIONS

1 Read **Hitler's talents** and **Hitler becomes leader** on page 24.

    a What changes did Hitler make to the DAP?

    b How was Hitler able to become party leader?

2 Read **Hitler and the SA** and **Why men joined the SA** on pages 24 and 25. What was the job of the SA?

3 Read pages 25–6.

    a Briefly say what happened in the Munich *Putsch*.

    b Was the *Putsch* (uprising) a success?

How do we know?

Hitler wrote two books. One was *Mein Kampf* ('My Struggle'). This was published in 1924. The other was called the 'Second Book'. It was not published until after Hitler died. There are also copies of speeches and conversations, and official Party papers.

Source A

▲ Burning of Jews in medieval Germany (from Schedal's *Chronicle*).

Hitler's two main ideas

1 Hatred of the Jews or anti-semitism.

Hitler hated the Jews. This is called anti-semitism. It was not new. For instance hatred of the Jews had been very strong in the Middle Ages (see Source A). In some sections of society this hatred had continued into the modern period.

2 The master race

There was a long standing belief in the master race and the superman. In the 19th century Charles Darwin wrote a book called *Origin of the Species*. Part of what he said was that some types of animals and plants do well and survive. Some fail and die out. This idea was adopted by some non-scientists and applied to humans.

The **Social Darwinists**, as they came to be called, said that some humans do well and some fail and that this was the result of a long and continuing struggle. Hitler (and many others) said that Germans were the humans who did well. They were superior and would survive. This idea was dangerous. It might allow everyone who was not of the German race to be wiped out. (The Jews were just one group among many considered inferior.)

Source B

Are You Blond?
If so, You are
A CULTURE–CREATOR
and
CULTURE–SUPPORTER

▲ The first page of a pamphlet written in 1913.

The party programme: Nationalism and Socialism

The first official description of the policy of the German Workers' Party was the *Twenty-Five Point Programme* of 1920. Source C on page 28 shows part of the programme of the DAP (Nazis).

Source C

1 We demand the union of all Germans in a Greater Germany.

2 We demand equal rights for Germany when dealing with other nations.

3 We demand more land for our growing population to live on.

4 Only those of German blood can belong to the German nation. No Jew may belong.

● ● ●

7 The State must give jobs to everyone.

8 Non-Germans cannot be allowed to live in Germany.

● ● ●

10 Every citizen must work.

11 No one should receive money without working.

12 No one is allowed to make money out of war.

13 All businesses should be run by the state.

14 We demand that big companies share out the profits.

15 We demand more old age pensions.

● ● ●

21 The government must improve the nation's health by looking after mothers and children.

22 We demand ....the formation of a people's army.

23 Newspapers which do not publish the ideas of the state must be forbidden.

● ● ●

25 We demand a strong, central government for Germany.

◄ **Extracts from the Twenty-Five Point Programme of the Nazi Party. It was originally drawn up by the DAP in February 1920.**

Nationalism. In Source C the nationalist ideas are those to do with the importance of the army, power, getting more land and race.

Socialism. In Source C the socialist ideas are those to do with controlling the way people lived and the economy of the country.

Hitler goes even further

Hitler soon went further than the ideas in the party programme shown in Source C. His speeches made reference to the struggles between strong and weak (see Source E).

Source D

Now we can say that the struggle for existence is the 'survival of the fittest' or the 'victory of the best'. The fittest... are the best.
Thousands of good and beautiful animals and plants have died out during the last forty eight million years, because they had to make room for other stronger and better animals and plants... Precisely the same applies to the history of nations.

▲ **Adapted from a book by Ernst Haeckel, 1900. Haeckel believed in 'Social Darwinism'.**

Source E

All of nature is one great struggle between strength and weakness, an eternal victory for the strong over the weak.

▲ **From a speech by Hitler in 1923.**

The strong were the 'culture creators' whose duty was to destroy all others (see Source B). Hitler said the Germans, or **Aryans**, were the master race. The best of these had blond hair, blue eyes and were very strong. They should prepare to take land from the 'lesser' races of eastern Europe.

Hitler's hatred of the Jews

Hitler's hatred of the Jews was based on **prejudice** (thinking bad of someone without any good reasons). Hitler blamed the Jews for unemployment, and Germany's economic trouble. He said they supported the Weimar Republic which had stabbed the German army in the back in 1918.

Hitler's message

Hitler's message to the German people was clear. They were the master race. They could take land and anything else they wanted from lower races. They could blame all their problems on the lesser races, especially the Jews.

QUESTIONS

1 Read **The Party Programme: Nationalism and Socialism** on page 27 and look at Source C.

   a Put a heading **Nationalism**. Make a list of three points which are to do with Nationalism.

   b Put a heading **Socialism**. Make a list of three points which are to do with Socialism.

2 Read **Hitler goes even further**. Who did Hitler believe to be the master race?

3 Read **Hitler's hatred of the Jews**.

   a What is prejudice?

   b What did Hitler say about the Jewish people?

Source F

THE ANTI-JEWS WANT TO WAKE YOU UP WORKERS, CITIZENS, SOLDIERS, WOMEN! SUPPORT US! for:

Who are the big capitalists [rich men]?
The Jews!

Who has made themselves lots of money?
The Jews!

Who led and paid the rebels against the government?
The Jews!

Who is the separate race within... our people?
The Jews!

Who offers you truly filthy art in the cinema, cabaret and theatre and wants Christian ideas to go to the devil?
The Jews!

▲ From a Nazi leaflet, printed in 1922.

Source G

All great cultures of the past were destroyed only because the originally creative race died from blood poisoning.
Therefore he who would live, let him fight. He who will not fight does not deserve to live.

▲ From Hitler's *Mein Kampf*, 1925.

Source H

Germany shall turn away from world trade and instead concentrate all its forces on providing our nation with enough living space. Such space can only be in the east.

▲ Adapted from Hitler's *Second Book*, written in 1928, but not published until 1959.

Hitler changes his plan of action

Hitler wanted power. Hitler also wanted to change Germany. His plan of action (strategy) as the leader of the Nazi Party was going to have to change after the failure of the Munich *Putsch* (revolt).

Losing the revolution

Hitler thought he would come to power by leading armed soldiers in a revolution. But the Munich *Putsch* did not work. Hitler was put in prison. He decided he had to change his ideas. He decided he would win power legally by winning votes in elections. The Nazi revolution would be introduced after he had won power.

Winning the votes

Hitler decided that when he came out of prison he had to build up the Nazi Party. The Nazis had to be so well organized and so attractive that the German people would vote them into power.

Reorganizing the Nazi Party from 1924

Hitler came out of prison in 1924. He set about reorganizing the Nazi Party. He set up branches all over Germany. Each branch (*Gau*) had its own leader (a party official called the *Gauleiter*). The SA was made stronger and more young men were brought into the party and the movement.

Rivals to Hitler

In northern Germany **Joseph Goebbels** and **Gregor Strasser** wanted to base the Nazi Party more on the support of the working classes and make it more socialist. Hitler called a Party Conference in Bamberg in Bavaria in 1926. He completely won over Goebbels who became a strong supporter of Hitler from then on. He was made Gauleiter of Berlin.

Source A

Instead of working to achieve power by an armed revolt, we will have to hold our noses and enter the Reichstag against Catholic and Marxist [communist] members. If outvoting them takes longer than outshooting them...at least sooner or later we shall have a majority and after that – Germany!

▲ From a letter written by Hitler while in prison in 1924.

Source B

During this period leaders whose views were still rooted in the pre-war days steadily disappeared. Their places were taken by young men of what was known as the front generation of 25–35 years old.

▲ Albert Krebs, a Gauleiter in Hamburg.

NATIONAL SOZIALIST

ODER UMSONST WAREN DIE OPFER

▲ A Nazi election poster of 1928. It says that the sacrifices made by Germany in the First World War were in vain.

Nazi successes 1925–28

1 The party was better organized after 1925.
2 Goebbels improved the propaganda (publicity) by producing posters like Source C.
3 The party was active throughout the whole of Germany, not just Bavaria.
4 The Nazis started to get support from people like farmers and skilled workers.
5 They had a remarkable leader in Hitler.

Nazis failures 1925–28

1 The Nazis still did badly in the elections to the Reichstag (see chart on the right).
2 Many Germans were not that interested in Nazi ideas.

Source D

The election results from the countryside show that with less effort and expense they get better results there than in the big cities.

▲ Adapted from the *Munich Observer* (a Nazi newspaper) just after the Reichstag election in 1928.

Source E

This is the great secret of our movement: an utter devotion to the idea of National Socialism...combined with a deep love of our leader who is the shining hero of the new freedom fighters.

▲ A glowing description of Hitler in an article written by Gregor Strasser in 1927. Strasser was later to come into conflict with Hitler, and was murdered by the SS in 1934.

Date	Nazi seats	Number of parties with more seats
1924 [May]	32	5
1924 [Dec.]	14	7
1928	12	7

▲ The Nazi Party's performance in Reichstag elections, 1924–8.

A lot of Germans were more contented during this time under Gustav Streseman (see pages 14–15). It was going to take a major upheaval to persuade people to vote for the Nazis.

And this is precisely what happened in 1929. There was a major economic upheaval. Hitler and the Nazis got their chance.

Source A

Unsere letzte Hoffnung: HITLER

▲ *Our Last Hope: Hitler*, a Nazi poster of 1932.

Source B

The victory of the national socialist movement will mean the overcoming of the old class spirit. It will train the nation to have iron determination. It will overcome democracy and make personality important.

▲ Adapted from the *Nazi Party Manifesto* 1930.

The economic crisis of 1929

The Weimar Republic (German government) could not cope with the economic crisis in 1929 (see pages 18–19). Many businesses went bankrupt. Many people lost their jobs. The Reichstag was helpless and President Hindenburg ruled by emergency powers.

Rise of the Nazi Party

In 1928 the Nazi party only had 12 seats in the Reichstag. By 1932 they were winning about 200 seats.

Hitler toured all over Germany by air and spoke to huge meetings of people in halls and in sports stadia. There were always spectacular processions and marches. Hitler decided to aim for the top political post. He challenged Hindenburg for the Presidency in 1932.

Hitler lost the election to be President, but he managed to get himself made Chancellor in 1933.

Why did more and more people vote for Hitler?

The economic crisis undoubtedly helped the Nazi Party. But the Nazis also made the most of the situation.

- Hitler made sure he appealed to **nationalism** (the Germans' love of Germany as one country).

- He also appealed deliberately to all the different social groups within Germany, from the working classes to the rich people.

Hitler's appeal to nationalism

1 Many Germans lost their jobs in the economic crisis. Hitler blamed the Weimar Republic for the crisis. He said he was Germany's last hope (see Source A). He would unite all Germans and make Germany rich and strong again.

2 Hitler revived talk of the 'stab in the back'. He said the German army had not been beaten in the war. It had been betrayed by the Weimar politicians. They were the ones who surrendered, not the army. He reminded the German people that the Treaty of Versailles was hateful. It had given German money and land to the Allies. Germany must have revenge.

3 He accused the Jews of being responsible for all Germany's problems. In this way he gave the Germans someone to blame for everything that went wrong.

Source C

Kopf-u.Handarbeiter wählt: Völkischen Block

▲ A Nazi anti-Jewish poster, published before Hitler came to power in 1933.

Source D

The National Socialist movement, assembled at this hour, as a fighting squad around its leader, today calls on the entire German people to join its ranks, and to pave a path that will bring Adolf Hitler to the head of the nation and thus

Lead Germany to Freedom

Hitler is the password of all who believe in Germany's resurrection. Hitler is the last hope of those who were deprived of everything: of farm and home, of savings, unemployment, survival.
. . . Hitler is the word of deliverance for millions, for they are in despair.

Hitler was bequeathed the legacy of two million dead comrades of the World War, who died not for the present system of the gradual destruction of our nation, but for Germany's future.

HITLER WILL WIN, BECAUSE THE PEOPLE WANT HIS VICTORY!

▲ An article from the *Munich Observer*, March 1932, supporting Hitler in the presidential elections.

Source E

GERMAN FARMER YOU BELONG TO HITLER! WHY?

The German farmer stands between two great dangers: One is the American system of Big capitalism! The other is the communist system. Big Capitalism and Communism work hand in hand: they serve the master plan of Jews the world over. Who alone can rescue the farmer from these dangers? NATIONAL SOCIALISM.

▲ Adapted from a Nazi leaflet, 1932.

Hitler's appeal to different groups

Hitler found something to appeal to all sections of German society.

1 The working class. The working class was the biggest single group in Germany. Hitler knew how important it was to have their support. He promised:
- better rights for working people
- to create more jobs.

Hitler said that the workers must follow the discipline of the Nazi party not trade unions.

2 The middle class. The old middle class were farmers, skilled workers and shopkeepers. The new middle class were office workers, civil servants and teachers. Both the old and the new middle class were afraid of the communists on the one hand and of the capitalists (big business) on the other. Hitler promised to protect them from both communism and capitalism.

3 The upper classes. These were the rich land owners or business people. Hitler played on their fears of Communism. He promised Germany would be rich and strong. The upper classes liked Hitler for attacking the Treaty of Versailles (which had given German money and land to the Allies).

4 Women. Many women voted according to their social position. But Hitler was especially keen to win their vote. He promised:
- to make the family more important.
- to give women a special place as wives and mothers.

Source F

▲ A Nazi Party poster, claiming that it protects the community. It advises families to contact their local Party organization if they need help.

Source G

GERMAN WOMEN!
GERMAN WOMEN!
Our young people defiled
The Welfare Minister has said that in a German School for Girls, 63 per cent of girls had experienced sexual intercourse and 47 per cent had some form of sexual disease. Our young people have been exposed to a flood of muck and filth, in print, in the theatre and in the cinema. This is the work of the Communists. They are destroying the family.

Must our young people sink into muck and filth? No!!! The National Socialists must win the election so they can stop this Communist work. So that once again women are honoured and valued.

◀ Adapted from a Nazi leaflet for the Reichstag elections, 1932.

Who changed parties to vote for the Nazis?

Look at the chart at the bottom of the page.

- Many Catholics supported the Centre Party (Z). Hitler's ideas did not appeal strongly to them. They preferred moderate policies (see Source H).

- The Communist Party (KPD) gained support. Certainly Communists were not being converted to Nazism. Hitler said the Communists were the enemy of Germany.

- Many working-class people supported the Social Democrats (SPD). The SPD lost some support but it did not collapse. Perhaps some workers turned to Nazism but some also turned to Communism. The workers may not have liked Hitler's attacks on trade unions.

- The middle classes mostly supported the Democrats (DDP) and the People's Party (DVP). By 1932 both these parties had collapsed. The middle classes were voting for the Nazis. They probably turned to Hitler because they had lost jobs and savings in the economic crisis.

- The upper classes and some of the middle classes supported the Nationalist Party (DNVP). The Nationalist Party lost votes to the Nazis. Hitler had taken many Nationalist ideas (such as dislike of the Treaty of Versailles). Hitler said he would make Germany rich and strong again. This appealed to big businessmen.

▲ An election poster from the 1920s. It reads, 'Women and men, ensure the happiness of your family and children by voting for the Christian People's Party' (Centre Party).

▲ A poster of 1932, showing what the Social Democrats believed the Nazis meant to the worker.

Party	May 1928	Sept 1930	July 1932	Nov 1932
Nazis (NSDAP)	12	107	230	196
National (DNVP)	73	41	37	52
People's (DVP)	45	30	7	11
Centre (Z)	62	68	75	70
Democrats (DDP)	25	20	4	2
Social Democrats (SPD)	153	143	133	121
Communists (KPD)	54	77	89	100

Reichstag election results, 1928–32 (number of seats won by the main parties).

► *The real meaning of the Hitler salute,*
by the artist, John Heartfield, 1932.
Heartfield, a communist, was commenting
on the fact that businesses were giving
money to the Nazi Party.

DER SINN DES
HITLERGRUSSES:

Motto:
MILLIONEN
STEHEN
HINTER MIR!

Kleiner Mann bittet um große Gabe

Although many upper-class people
looked down on Hitler, they saw he was
a strong leader and could be useful to
them. They made the mistake of thinking
they could control him.

Did Hitler really have the support of the German people?

Look at the chart below right. Hitler
never gained more than about one third
(33 per cent) of all the votes cast.
Therefore more people were against the
Nazis in 1932, than were for them.

The importance of the middle classes to Hitler

The chart on page 35
shows the collapse of the
middle-class parties (the
DDP and the DVP). The
middle-class vote
switched to Hitler.
Furthermore, most active
members of the Nazi
Party were middle class.
(look at the chart below.)

Party	May 1928	Sept 1930	July 1932	Nov 1932
Nazis (NSDAP)	2.6	18.3	37.4	33.1
National (DNVP)	14.2	7.0	5.9	8.8
People's (DVP)	8.7	4.5	1.2	1.9
Centre's (Z)	12.1	11.8	12.5	11.9
Democrats (DDP)	4.9	3.8	1.0	1.0
Social Democrats (SPD)	29.8	24.5	21.6	20.4
Communists (KPD)	10.6	13.1	14.3	16.9

▲ Reichstag election results,
1928–32 (percentage of the vote
received by each of the main
parties).

Category	% of Nazi Party	% of German society
Working class	28.1	45.9
Middle class of which:	66.9	35.8
White-collar workers	25.6	12.0
Self-employed	20.7	9.0
Civil servants	6.6	4.2
Small farmers	14.0	10.6

◄ A comparison between
working-class and middle-class
membership of the Nazi Party
in 1930.

Source K

I have personally given one million marks to the Nazi Party...Just before the Nazis seized power the big businesses began to give money to the Nazi Party... In all, the amounts given by heavy industry to the Nazis were about two million marks a year.

▲ From Fritz Thyssen, *I Paid Hitler*, 1941.

QUESTIONS

1 a Make a larger copy of the chart below.

Group	What Hitler promised
Working class	
Middle class	
Upper class	
Women	

  b Complete the chart by writing in what Hitler promised each group.

2 Read **Who changed parties to vote for the Nazis?** on page 35.

  a Which two classes gave most support to the Nazis?
  b Why did many working-class people stay with the Social Democrats?

2.5 Hitler's rise to power: a summary

This summary looks at two key questions.

1 How important was Hitler in the rise of the Nazis?

Without Hitler there would have been no Nazi movement and no Nazi government in 1933. Even though Hitler was an outstanding leader, other factors also helped his rise to power.

● **Hitler's talents**
  a From the early 1920s, Hitler said that a strong leader was important. When he established absolute control of the Nazi Party he was carrying out the *Führer Prinzip* or **leadership principle**. He carried this principle forward to be a dictator when he achieved power in Germany.

  b Hitler was a brilliant speaker and very good at designing publicity for the Party.

c He made the decisions about how to gain power. Before 1923, he was going to overthrow the Weimar Republic in an armed uprising. When this failed, he changed his ideas and decided the Nazi party would gain power legally through elections. Only then would the Nazis change Germany.

● **Hitler's support from other people**
Rudolf Hess was Hitler's loyal deputy in the 1920s. **Gregor Strasser** and **Joseph Goebbels** supported Hitler in the north of Germany. **Ernst Röhm** ran the SA. He made sure that anyone who opposed Hitler and the Nazis would be threatened with violence.

● **Other things which helped Hitler**
The state of Germany between 1929 and 1933 also helped Hitler seize power (see page 38).

2 Why had Hitler come to power by 1933, but not by 1929?

We need to look back over the stages of Germany's history from 1918 to 1933.

- **1918–23** Germany had lost the First World War. The Treaty of Versailles (1919) made Germany give land and money to the Allies. All the money flowing out of Germany to the Allies created inflation at home. Businesses were ruined. People lost their jobs.

- **1923–1929** The USA set up the Dawes Plan. By this plan Germany did not have to pay out so much money to the Allies straight away. The USA invested money in German businesses. The result was that there were many more jobs. This made the German people more contented with the government. Stresemann was successful in managing the parties in the Reichstag and improving Germany's standing abroad. Most people were not interested in Hitler's extreme ideas.

- **1929–1933** The Wall Street Crash in the USA meant that the USA pulled money out of Germany. This led to a serious economic crisis. Many businesses collapsed. Millions of people lost their jobs.

People became more and more discontented with the government. The moderate parties of the government could not agree on how to deal with all the problems. The Chancellors made more and more use of the emergency powers. They ruled without the Reichstag, so democracy was gradually replaced by dictatorship. This was Hitler's chance.

The Nazis had reorganized themselves and changed their tactics. They had promises for everyone. People suffering from poverty and depression voted for Hitler. In July 1932 the Nazis became the largest party in the Reichstag. They did not have an overall majority, and the politicians gave Hitler power thinking they would be able to control him.

SUMMARY

The rise of Hitler

- ► **1914** Enlisted in German army.
- ► **1919** Joined the DAP.
- ► **1920** Placed in charge of propaganda. Helped draw up the Party Programme.
- ► **1921** Displaced Drexler as Party leader. Renamed the Party the NSDAP (Nazi Party). Set up the SA.
- ► **1923** Attempted to seize power through the Munich *Putsch*.
- ► **1924–5** In Landsberg Prison. Wrote the first part of *Mein Kampf*.
- ► **1925** Refounded Party and adopted 'legal' policy.
- ► **1926** Won over Goebbels and Strasser.
- ► **1928** The Nazis won 107 seats in the Reichstag.
- ► **1932** Nazis largest party in the Reichstag. In March Hitler lost the presidential election to Hindenburg.
- ► **1933** Hitler appointed Chancellor by Hindenburg.

Exercise: Appealing to the masses

Hitler was a brilliant speaker. Do Sources 3 and 4 support this view? Explain your answers.

Why did the Nazi Party organize such huge rallies?

Read pages 37–8.
a What were Hitler's talents as a leader?
b What other reasons were there for his rise to power?

Source 1

Fifth-formers [15-16 year-olds] are not really much bothered with the study of Hitler's thoughts; it is simply something that makes the blood rush through one's veins and gives the idea that something great is under way, the roaring of a stream which one does not wish to escape.

▲ **From a Protestant church report, 1931.**

Source 2

Hitler arriving to speak at a mass rally.

Source 3

The hall was a sea of brightly coloured flags. Even Hitler's arrival was made dramatic. The band stopped playing. There was a hush over 30,000 people packed in the hall. Then the band struck up the *Badenweiler March*, a very catchy tune. Hitler appeared. . .strode slowly down the long centre aisle while 30,000 hands were rasied in salute. . .In such an atmosphere no wonder. . . that every word dropped by Hitler seemed like an inspired word from on high . . . every lie told is accepted as high truth itself.

▲ **William Shirer, an American journalist, who watched Hitler speak in September 1934.**

Source 4

As the spirit moves him, he is promptly changed into one of the greatest speakers of the century. Adolf Hitler enters a hall. He sniffs the air. For a minute he gropes, feels his way, senses the atmosphere. Suddenly he bursts forth. His words go like an arrow to their target, telling the crowd what it most wants to hear.

Otto Strasser, a Nazi who disliked Hitler as a person, writing about his expertise as a speaker.

Source 5

People in a crowd can sacrifice their own self-interest, personal beliefs and standards. They are easily affected by suggestions. Individuals can therefore lose their identity and become part of the mass identity.

▲ **A French psychologist in the late 19th century, explaining how people in crowds will believe things and do things they would not do on their own.**

CHAPTER 3

THE NAZI RÉGIME 1933–45

This chapter deals with the Nazi revolution. First it explains what the Nazi revolution means, then it tells how the state moved from a democracy to a dictatorship and finally to a military machine.

3.1 What was the Nazi revolution?

Hitler became Chancellor in 1933. From 1933 to 1934, he worked to change the German government into a **dictatorship** by using the legal powers of the Constitution as laid down by the Weimar Republic. This was called the 'legal' revolution.

Then Hitler and the Nazis worked to make this dictatorship permanent. This was called the 'national' revolution. The 'legal' and the 'national' revolutions together made up the Nazi revolution.

3.2 The 'legal' revolution

Even though Hitler was made Chancellor in 1933, President Hindenburg was still in charge. Also Hitler was only head of a **coalition** government. If the other parties in the coalition disagreed with him Hitler could not overrule them. Hitler wanted to rule by himself without Hindenburg or any other party in his way.

Source A

▲ Hindenburg making Hitler Chancellor, January 1933.

Party	Seats
Nazis (NSDAP)	288
National (DNVP)	52
Centre (Z)	74
Social Democrats (SPD)	120
Communists (KPD)	81

▲ The results of the Reichstag election of 5 March 1933 (number of seats won).

Calling an election

Hitler asked Hindenburg to call an election. It was set for 5 March 1933. Hitler did a number of things in the hope that the Nazis would gain a majority. In the lead up to the election Hitler asked Hindenburg to declare a **state of emergency**. This was used to stop other parties (particularly the Social Democrats and the Communists) from having meetings and getting people to vote for them.

Hitler's excuse for asking for the state of emergency was the **burning of the Reichstag** building on 27 February 1933. Hitler immediately blamed the Communists. Certainly a Dutch Communist was caught but no one is sure whether it was a Communist plot or even whether the Nazis burnt it down themselves. It provided the Nazis with a good chance to attack Communism.

The result of the election

Look at the chart at the bottom of page 40. The Nazis still only had less than half the total seats. To change the Constitution (and create a Nazi dictatorship) they needed two-thirds of the seats.

How did Hitler win a two-thirds majority in the Reichstag?

Hitler did two things. He said there was an emergency and the Communists must not take their seats. This cut out 81 MPs (see chart). Then Hitler gained the support of the Centre Party (Z) by promising them that he would look after the Catholic Church in Germany.

Changing the Constitution – March 1933

Having kept out the Communists and made a deal with the Centre Party to vote for him, Hitler had a two-thirds majority in the Reichstag. He brought in the **Enabling Law**. This made it possible for Hitler to make his own laws without the Reichstag.

▲ The Reichstag building on fire, 27 February 1933.

Source C

The Reichstag has passed the following law, and it is now proclaimed:

Article 1
In addition to the passing of laws in the constitutional houses... the government is also able to pass laws.

Article 3
The laws passed by the government shall be issued by the Chancellor and published in the official paper.

▲ From the Enabling Law, 1933.

Source D

▲ 'They salute with both hands now!' A cartoon by the British cartoonist, David Low, on the treatment of the SA in the Night of the Long Knives, 1934.

Hitler brought in another law which made the Nazi Party the only party in Germany. Hitler had made Germany into a dictatorship. And he had done it legally. Hitler now wanted to become President instead of Hindenburg. He needed the German army on his side. So he decided to please the army by breaking the power of its rivals, Ernst Röhm and the SA. In the **Night of the Long Knives** Hitler used the SS (see page 46) to kill Röhm and other SA leaders.

Hitler as Führer

When Hindenburg died in 1934, Hitler put the job of Chancellor and President together. The army swore an oath of personal loyalty to Hitler (see Source F). He now called himself the **Führer**.

Source E

The government has passed the following law, which is:

Article 1
The only political party in Germany is the National Socialist German Workers' Party.

▲ From The Law against the New Formation of Parties, July 1933.

Source F

I swear before God to give my unconditional obedience to Adolf Hitler, Führer of the Reich and of the German people. I give my word as a brave soldier to keep this oath ... even at the peril of my life.

▲ From the army's oath of loyalty to Hitler, taken from 1934 onwards.

Source G

▲ The Reichstag chamber in the early 1930s before Hitler came to power.

▲ The Reichstag chamber in 1939.

ERNST RÖHM (1887–1934)

Röhm led the *Sturm Abteilung* (SA). By the 1930s, he was worried that the SS (see page 46) was becoming more and more powerful. When Hitler came to power Röhm wanted Hitler to allow the SA to take over the German army. This would increase Röhm's power. Instead Hitler stood by the German army. He used the SS to kill Röhm and many other SA leaders on the night of 30 June 1934. The night became known as the **Night of the Long Knives**. The power of the SA was broken.

QUESTIONS

1 Read pages 40–42. Put a heading **The 'legal' revolution**. Write out the following events in the **correct order** to show how Hitler came to power:

• **2nd August 1934** Death of Hindenburg. Hitler becomes Führer.

• **30th June 1934** Night of the Long Knives.

• **24 March 1933** Enabling Act passed.

• **27 February 1933** Reichstag set on fire.

• **14th July 1933** Nazis ban all other parties.

• **5 March 1933** Nazis win election.

3.3 How did the Nazis enforce their political power?

The 'national' revolution

After the 'legal' revolution came the 'national' revolution. This aimed to make Germany into a **totalitarian** state. Everybody would be controlled by the government.

How did Hitler gain total control?

Hitler used two methods to control the German people. One was **propaganda**. The other was **terror**.

The first method – propaganda

Propaganda comes from the word 'propagate'. Propagate means to spread. The Nazis had very firm ideas which they wanted spread to the German people.

Source **A**

Propaganda must confine itself to a very few points and repeat them endlessly.

▲ Adolf Hitler, *Mein Kampf*, 1925.

Source **B**

It is not enough for people to be more or less content with our government... Rather we want to work on people until they have given in to us...The new Ministry has no other aim than to unite the German nation behind the ideal of the national revolution.

▲ Adapted from part of a speech by Goebbels to a press conference, March 1933.

Hitler set out the best way of doing this (see Source A). Spreading a few ideas very often is called **indoctrination**. Indoctrination also means squeezing out all other ideas.

The Ministry for People's Enlightenment and Propaganda – 1933

This was set up under the control of **Dr Joseph Goebbels**. He aimed to make every German person think the same way – the Nazi way (see Source B). The Ministry set up several departments. One of these was the Reich Chamber of Culture.

The Reich Chamber of Culture

This was sub-divided into six sections which controlled the information in its own area of culture.

Source **C**

Ganz Deutschland hört den Führer

mit dem Volksempfänger

▲ A Nazi poster from the 1930s, showing the importance of radio. The slogan says 'All of Germany listens to the Führer on national radio'.

JOSEPH GOEBBELS (1897–1945)

Goebbels joined the Nazi Party in 1922. He became head of propaganda and was elected to the Reichstag in 1930. When Hitler came to power in 1933, Goebbels was made the Minister for Enlightenment and Propaganda.

He was a brilliant speaker, with an excellent voice. He was particularly good at presenting Nazi policies on the radio. During the Second World War (1939–45) he made some famous speeches to keep up the morale of the German people.

He was viciously anti-Jewish and totally devoted to Hitler. He committed suicide the day after Hitler in April 1945.

Source D

I consider radio to be the most modern and important instrument for influencing people. I also believe that ... radio will, in the end, replace newspapers...At all costs avoid being boring. I put that before everything. You must....bring forth a nationalist culture....to suit the pace of modern life.

▲ Goebbels talking to the controllers of German radio, March 1933.

These six sections included the Press Chamber, the Radio Chamber, the Theatre Chamber and later the Film Chamber. Through these chambers Goebbels could control all the information that went out to the German people.

The Press Chamber and The Radio Chamber

Goebbels told the Press Chamber to have regular meetings with the newspaper journalists. In this way the Press Chamber instructed the newspapers what to say.

Goebbels was one of the first people to realize how important the radio was. More Germans owned radios in the 1930s than even the Americans owned. With a radio in nearly every home the Radio Chamber could control everything that people heard.

Source E

In the next issue there must be a lead article in which the decision of the Führer, no matter what it will be, will be discussed as the only correct one for Germany.

▲ General Instruction No. 674 given to the press by the Ministry for People's Enlightenment and Propaganda.

Schools and Universities

Schools and universities were told what to teach. Therefore children learnt only one way of looking at things. Books were **censored** and libraries were burnt.

The second method – Terror

The second method that Hitler used to control the German people was terror. Goebbels knew that some people would not believe the propaganda. They would have to be frightened. If that did not work they would have to be put in camps or killed.

Who carried out the terror?

- **The SS (*Schutzstaffel*)**. The SS was set up in 1925 as part of the SA. They wore black shirts and were very carefully disciplined. In 1934 they replaced the SA as the most important armed group in the country. Gradually the SS split into three sections. One section looked after security. Another section was the *Waffen* SS – providing the top units in the army. The final section was the 'death's head units'. They ran the concentration camps during the Second World War.

Source **G**

Any attempt to put forward, or even hold different ideas [from Hitler's] will be ruthlessly dealt with as something which threatens the unity of the [German] state. The duty of the political police is to discover, watch and render harmless the enemies of the state.

▲ **Instructions to the Gestapo (the secret police).**

Source **H**

Justice is no aim in itself. It is there to keep order... It is not the task of justice to be mild or tough. Its task simply is to serve that purpose [keeping law and order in the German state].

▲ **From *Hitler's Table-Talk*, 1942. This book was a record of Hitler's conversations which were noted down by his staff.**

Source **I**

Justice is that which is useful to the German people.

▲ **Judge Roland Freisler (1893–1945). Freisler joined the Nazi Party in 1925, and remained a loyal supporter until his death in 1945.**

Source **F**

▲ The core of the SS. Himmler, their leader, is third from the right at the front.

- **The Gestapo**. The Gestapo was the Secret Police Force. It was led by **Reynhard Heydrich** who was utterly ruthless. The Gestapo's job was to crush anyone who was against Hitler (see Source G).

- **Justice and the law courts**. In a democracy the law protects ordinary people. Justice is above politics. Hitler changed all this. In 1934 he set up the **People's Court**. In this court people were tried for speaking out against Hitler. Between 1934 and 1939, 534 people were executed for speaking out against Hitler.

- **The concentration camps**. The SA and the SS ran concentration camps – large prisons where life was harsh. Anyone the Nazis did not like was sent there including Communists, homosexuals, Jews and anyone who had spoken against Hitler.

The first camp was at **Dachau**. But many others followed. During the Second World War some camps became extermination camps.

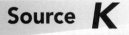
Source J

Tolerance means weakness. In the light of this meaning, punishment will be mercilessly handed out whenever the interest of the fatherland dictates it.

Anyone who discusses politics, carries on controversial talks and meetings, forms groups, loiters around with others will be hanged.

▲ **From the Regulations of Dachau Concentration Camp, 1933.**

HIMMLER AND HEYDRICH

Heinrich Himmler and Reynhard Heydrich were probably the two most feared men in Germany.

Himmler led the SS and became very powerful after the Night of the Long Knives when many SA leaders were killed.

He went on to control the Gestapo as well as the SS. He was also in charge of the extermination camps where six million people died. He committed suicide in 1945.

Heydrich was made head of the Gestapo in 1936. He was Himmler's deputy. He also helped to organize the extermination camps which included Dachau, Buchenwald and Ravensbruck (see map on page 83). He was assassinated in 1942.

Source K

▲ **Political prisoners in Dachau concentration camp in 1933.**

The Nazis seemed to gain control of the German people easily. However, there were many people who did not like what the Nazis were doing. We will look at the different groups of people who opposed the Nazis and ask three questions. Then we can see how these questions are answered at the end of page 51.

- In what ways did these people oppose the Nazis?

- What did the Nazis do about people who opposed them?

- How successful were people who opposed the Nazis?

Political parties and Hitler

The Social Democrats (SPD) and the Communists (KPD) both spoke out against Hitler. By 1933 Hitler had got the Communists banned from the Reichstag (after the Reichstag fire).

Voting on the Enabling Law 1933

The Social Democrats turned up to the Reichstag session at the Opera House (because of the fire). They wanted to vote against the Enabling Law which would give Hitler enormous power. Men from the SA surrounded the building and jostled the members. Goering watched through binoculars to see how the members voted. It was difficult not to be scared.

Source A

▲ Forty thousand workers being presented to Hitler for inspection at a Nuremberg rally.

Source B

At the beginning of 1936 the Communists switched to propaganda by word of mouth… It is clear that the Communist propaganda was having some success in some factories…

The SPD [Social Democrats] have worked mainly by giving out news and… setting up groups in factories, sports clubs and other organisations.

▲ Extracts from a Gestapo report about the secret work of the Social Democrats and the Communists, 1937.

Silencing the Social Democrats and the Communists

Shortly after the Enabling Law was passed by the Reichstag, Hitler banned both the Social Democrats and the Communists from being political parties at all. Both parties were driven underground and worked through the 1930s producing secret anti-Nazi propaganda in factories and other work places. However, the two parties had hated each other since 1919 and could not, even now in the common cause against Nazism, work together. They both fought for the support of the working class. Separately, they were ineffective and made the work of the Gestapo much easier.

Banning trade unions 1933

The next step was to ban trade unions. The Nazis then organized working people's lives in several ways.

- They set up the **National Labour Service** (RAD).

- They set up the **German Labour Front** (DAF). This said what hours should be worked.

- They set up **Beauty of Labour** (SDA) to improve working conditons.

- They set up **Strength through Joy** (KDF) to keep the workforce happy with leisure and sports clubs.

Most workers accepted that these new organizations had taken over from the old bargaining of the trade unions. It seemed to work well.

Source C

The Führer entrusted me with the job of getting rid of degenerate art from our museums... no fewer than 608 paintings of yours had to be seized...

The fact could leave no doubt in your mind that your paintings did not contribute to the advancement of German culture.

I hereby expel you from the National Chamber of Fine Arts and forbid you any activity in the field of graphic arts.

▲ Order from The National Chamber of Fine Arts forbidding Karl Schmidt-Rottluff, a well known artist, from painting.

Source D

The much praised 'academic freedom' shall be driven out of Germany's universities.

▲ Martin Heidegger, the famous philosopher, who was at the time Rector of the University of Freiburg, May 1933.

Writers, intellectuals, artists and Hitler

Some people felt that life was new and exciting under the Nazis. But many writers and artists felt that the Nazis stopped all freedom of speech. They were destroying the experiments in art under the Weimar Republic (see pages 16-17). Some spoke out. Some kept quiet. But they all got caught up in Goebbels' **Ministry of People's Enlightenment and Propaganda**. Some books and plays were banned. Films, radio, books, newspapers and even paintings were censored. Many writers, intellectuals and scientists left Germany.

Young people and Hitler

Hitler said it was very important to bring up children to believe in Nazi ideas. Hitler set up Youth Movements for boys and girls. In 1936 the **Law Concerning the Hitler Youth** was brought in. This was aimed at increasing the number of young people in the Hitler Youth Movement.

Many young people did join the Hitler Youth Movement. There were all sorts of sporting and leisure activities. But some young people would not join. Sometimes they belonged to Church groups. Sometimes they just liked to be different.

The churches and Hitler

At first the churches in Germany were pleased that the Nazis wanted to promote family values and good behaviour. Life under the Weimar Republic had seemed immoral to many Christians .

The Catholic Church

In 1933 the Catholic Church and Hitler signed an agreement. It said that the Church would let Hitler alone if he left the Church alone. However, the Nazis did not leave the Church alone. By 1941 the Catholic Church was speaking out against Hitler's abuse of human rights, particularly the killing of insane people.

The Protestant Churches

The Protestant Churches also became more and more unhappy with the way the Nazis treated people. By the end of the 1930s Hitler was trying to replace the Churches with a Faith Movement (controlled by the Nazis). It did not have much effect in the long run.

Source E

It is on our youth that the future of the German nation depends. We must prepare the whole of the German youth for its duties. The following law states:

Article 1
All the youth of Germany is to be organized in the Hitler Youth.

Article 2
It is not only in home and school, but in the Hitler Youth as well, that Germany's youth is to be educated physically, mentally and morally in the spirit of National Socialism to serve the nation.

▲ Taken from the Law Concerning the Hitler Youth, 1936.

▼ A poster by Ludwig Hohlwin, advertising the League of German Maidens in the Hitler Youth.

Source F

BUND DEUTSCHER MÄDEL IN DER HITLER JUGEND

Hitler and the army

Most soldiers swore the oath of loyalty to Hitler (see Source F on page 42). Hitler also did three things to make sure the army obeyed him:

1 The Nazi badge was added to the army uniform.
2 Part of the SS – the Waffen SS (see page 46) was put at the head of the German army to keep control.
3 In 1938 Hitler sacked a large number of generals. He set up a new high command with himself in overall control.

Even so some army officers were unhappy with the Nazi ideas. **General Ludwig Beck** (Chief of the General Staff) secretly asked Britain and France to oppose Hitler.

In what ways did people oppose Hitler?

The Social Democrats and Communists, some trade unionists and some army officers secretly worked against Hitler. Many writers and scientists left Germany. Some young people refused to join the Hitler Youth Movement. The Churches began to speak out against Hitler.

What did the Nazis do about people who opposed them?

The Nazis banned all political parties who by definition would hold different ideas to the Nazis. They banned trade unions. They banned books and literature which did not support Nazi ideas. They trained children to believe in all the Nazi ideas. Hitler made sure that the army obeyed him personally. The SS and the Gestapo tracked down anyone who opposed Nazi ideas. They sent thousands to concentration camps.

Source G

▲ Nazi banners in a Protestant church in Berlin, 1934.

Source H

We declare that the constitution of the German Evangelical [Protestant] Church has been destroyed. The men who have seized the church leadership have divorced themselves from the Christian Church.

▲ Protest by some Protestant bishops against those Protestants who had co-operated with the Nazis.

QUESTIONS

1 Which group might have been the most serious threat to Hitler if they had acted together to oppose him?

How successful were people who opposed the Nazis?

No-one was very successful until 1941 when Germany was doing badly in the war. Then the people who opposed Hitler began to work together against the Nazi régime.

Source A

Our nation's only true possession is its good blood.

▲ Walther Darré, German Food Minister. He wrote several books about racial ideas.

Source B

The first principle for us was and is the recognition of the values of blood and selection.

We sorted out the people whom we thought unsuitable for the formation of the SS simply on the basis of outward appearance.

▲ From a speech by Heinrich Himmler, head of the SS, 1935.

Source C

◀ A Nazi poster of 1938 showing the ideal Aryan family.

The ideas about race were the most important part of Nazi beliefs. There were two main policies:

1 To make a master race in Germany – the **Aryans**.
2 To destroy the Jews.

Making the master race

Hitler said that the Germans were Aryans. But Germany should have a policy of producing yet more pure Aryans. This could be done by **selective breeding**. In other words, preventing anyone who did not conform to the Aryan type from having children.

Selective breeding

The SS were part of the drive for selective breeding. The SS recruited men who were of Aryan blood. That is, they were tall, fair haired and blue or grey eyed. They could only marry women of Aryan blood.

There were **race farms** all over Germany for breeding Aryan children. Women of Aryan blood were brought to the farms and had children by SS fathers. This was one of the methods the Nazis used to make a pure Aryan master race.

Teaching about race

Race studies were taught in school. Children were told that only the 'best' people should be allowed to breed. Science teachers had to talk about race in Biology, Physics and Chemistry. Teachers who protested were stopped from teaching.

A child being examined to see if it has the correct Aryan looks.

The eternal God created for our nation a law that is peculiar to its own kind. It took shape in the Leader Adolf Hitler, and in the National Socialist [Nazi] state created by him.

▲ Orders from a German Christian group.

▼ The Nazis organized a 'shut out' of Jewish shops on 1 April 1933. The sign reads: 'Germans! Protect yourselves! Do not buy from Jews!' This SA man is making sure nobody enters this shop which is owned by a Jew.

Race and Religion

The Nazis tried to back up their ideas by saying that the Bible showed there were only two races. One was the Jews. The other was the Aryans. The Nazis said that God had a special purpose for the Aryans.

What happens when you build a master race?

This race policy of the Nazis was bound to lead to violence. The first form of violence was against 'inferior' races outside Germany. The master race needed their land.

The second form of violence was persecuting and getting rid of the 'inferior' races inside Germany. These were largely the Jews.

Persecuting the Jews

The Nazis started to persecute the Jews as soon as they came to power. In Germany there were three stages to this persecution (see page 54).

Deutsche!
Wehrt Euch!
Kauft nicht bei Juden!

Stage 1
No civil rights 1933–38

For these first five years the Nazis took away Jewish rights.

- No protection by the police.

- The SA were used to close Jewish shops.

- Jewish civil servants were sacked. (Hindenburg insisted they could keep their jobs if they had fought for Germany in the First World War.)

- Jews could not inherit land.

- Parks, restaurants, swimming baths and museums were closed to Jews.

- Marriage or sexual intercourse between Germans and Jews was forbidden.

Spreading hatred

Hatred for the Jews was spread in newspapers and in the classrooms (see Source I).

Source G

The victim's blood is tapped... the fresh [or powdered] blood of the slaughtered child is further used by Jews, by pregnant Jewesses, for circumcision.

▲ From a Nazi newspaper that deliberately spread lies about Jews.

Source H

Paragraph 1
Marriages between Jews and Citizens of German or kindred blood are hereby forbidden.

Paragraph 2
Extramarital intercourse between Jews and citizens of German or kindred blood is forbidden.

▲ Law for the Protection of German Blood and German Honour, 1935.

Source I

► Jewish schoolchildren being humiliated in front of their class.

Stage 2
More persecution 1938–41

From 1938 things grew worse for the Jews in Germany. The reason for this was that Hitler was in a stronger position in 1938 than he had been in 1933. Propaganda and terror had stopped people speaking out. Also Hitler had been successful abroad and knew that Britain and France would not do anything.

Crystal Night

This was a night in November 1938 when Jewish shops and synagogues were attacked all over Germany. It was called Crystal Night because of all the broken glass on the pavements next morning.

The attacks were probably organized by the SA on orders from Goebbels. But Goebbels said the German people had attacked the shops and synagogues because the Jews swindled them.

Even worse

From 1938 Jews had to wear badges (a yellow, six pointed star – see Source F). They could not run shops. They could not even choose their children's names. In some places they had to live in separate areas. These were called **ghettoes**.

Stage 3
The Holocaust 1941–45

From 1941 the Nazi plan was to exterminate the Jews. This **genocide** (mass destruction) was known as the Holocaust (see pages 83–6).

(see pages 83–6)

QUESTIONS

1 What were the two main Nazi ideas about race? (see page 52)

2 Give some examples of how the Jews were persecuted by the Nazis.

3 Why were cartoons like Source J produced by the Nazis?

Source J

▲ Anti-Jewish cartoon from a children's book, 1938.

The aim of the Nazis was to put forward the idea of the perfect master race. The purpose of culture was to promote the racial state. All paintings and sculpture should show the German people that the master race was great.

Weimar art and Nazi art

Some famous artists of the Weimar Republic were Paul Klee (see Source A), Ernst Barlach and Max Beckman. Their paintings were not approved of by the Nazis and were collected together in special exhibitions of 'degenerate' (low) art.

The artists at the time of the Weimar Republic believed in painting pictures about life as they saw it. Sometimes this was experimental and not necessarily realistic. Hitler said this was wrong. He said that art must serve the state. This meant that paintings must show strong men, ready to fight and women who could produce strong healthy babies. This was how the German people must see themselves.

Nazi artists

The best known Nazi artists were Arthur Kampf and Adolf Ziegler. They produced many paintings using the stories of old legends and myths.

Venus and Adonis by Arthur Kampf

This was one of the most famous paintings of the Nazi period (see Source B). It shows two figures from old myths but it was meant to inspire the German people. It shows all the important Nazi ideas about the master race:

- The man and the woman are strong and healthy.
- The man is armed and ready to fight.
- The horse behind him represents war.
- The woman is submissive and dependent on the man.

Is *Venus and Adonis* a good painting?

The painting fulfills Hitler's demands, but is it a good painting? In fact, it is badly painted and the figures are copied from other paintings. The woman is taken from Source C, the horse from Source D and the man's head from Source E. The much prized treasure of the new Nazi art was therefore a forgery!

▲ **Dancing with Fear, painted by Paul Klee in 1938.**

Source B

◄ *Venus and Adonis,* painted by Arthur Kampf in 1939.

▼ *Napoleon crossing the Alps* by Jacques-Louis David (1748–1825).

Source C

◄ *Venus and Adonis* by Titian (1487–1576).

Source D

▼ *The Creation of Adam* by Michelangelo (1475–1564).

Source E

▲ Architect's model of the People's Hall, Berlin.

Nazi architecture and the Third Reich

The Third Reich was what Hitler called Germany under his rule. He said it would last for a thousand years.

Hitler was interested in architecture. He wanted grand buildings that would also last for a thousand years. He made plans to rebuild Berlin.

The new Berlin or Germania

Hitler planned to rebuild Berlin by 1950. There would be huge buildings to show the power and strength of Germany.

In the centre of the city would be a People's Hall to hold 150,000 people.

He would rename the city Germania. It would show the power and greatness of Germany and the master race.

Nazi films

Hitler and Goebbels made full use of a new invention – films.

Hitler employed a brilliant actress and film director to make a record of life in Nazi Germany. The director was called **Leni Riefenstahl**. She filmed the mass rallies, marches and the 1936 Olympic Games.

► A model of the new city centre intended for Berlin, 1939.

en the clips were put together they made a film
ed *Triumph of the Will*. The film was shown all over
rmany. It encouraged all Germans to feel part of the
at new world of the Third Reich. Stills from this film
vide photographs today of some of the main events
he Third Reich.

ns on race

ns were also used to put across the Nazi ideas on
e and selective breeding. This was done by showing
t farmers only bred from the best animals and plants.
erefore, the Nazis said, Germans should only breed
n the best people. Many of the films were made to
ourage Germans to hate the Jews.

urce **H**

A religious procession
anized by the National
h Church. A still from the
paganda film, *Triumph of
Will*.

▼ A small section of a mass rally
showing the huge numbers attending.
A still from the propaganda film,
Triumph of the Will.

urce **I**

SUMMARY

1933

► Reichstag Fire.

► Enabling Act.

► Law against the New Formation of Parties.

► Ministry for People's Enlightenment and Propaganda set up.

► Gestapo set up.

► First concentration camps set up.

► National Labour Service (RAD) set up.

1934

► Night of the Long Knives.

► Hitler became Führer

1935

► Marriage illegal between German and Jew.

1936

► Gestapo merged with SS.

► Hitler Youth set up.

1938

► Crystal Night.

QUESTIONS

1 Read page 56. What was the purpose of art and architecture for the Nazis?

2 Read **The New Berlin or Germania** on page 58. Why did Hitler want to rebuild Berlin?

3 Read **Nazi Films**. How did the Nazis use films?

Hitler's aims in 1933

1 To pull Germany through the Depression and to create more jobs for Germans.
2 To produce more guns, tanks and aeroplanes to make Germany a great military power again.

Going slowly 1933–35

Hjalmar Schacht was in charge of the German economy. He wanted to make Germany rich again by increasing Germany's trade with less developed countries and strengthening the German currency. He did not want Germany to rearm (produce more weapons) too fast.

Source A

▲ An armaments factory in Düsseldorf in 1939.

Going faster 1935–40

Hitler did not want to wait. He thought Schacht was too slow. He wanted Germany to conquer other countries and take their land and money. He needed a big, well equipped army to carry out his plan.

Blitzkreig

Blitzkreig means 'lightning war'. Hitler said his plan was that the German army would strike like lightning and would conquer nearby countries one by one. Then Germany would have land or living space (*Lebensraum*) for German people. It would also have all the money from the conquered country's industries.

Four Year Plan 1936–40

Hitler sacked Schacht and made Goering head of his new Four Year Plan. This was a secret plan to make Germany ready for war in four years. Hitler also wanted to make sure that Germany did not rely on other countries for new materials – this policy was called **autarchy**.

Source B

If we do not succeed in bringing the German army as rapidly as possible to the rank of first army in the world, then Germany will be lost!

I set the following tasks:

i The German armed force must be operational within four years.

ii The German economy must be fit for war within four years.

▲ From Hitler's memorandum on the Four Year Plan, 1936.

The effect of the Four Year Plan

Two things made Hitler more confident. German factories made more and more guns, ships, tanks, bombs and aeoplanes. More and more young men joined the German army. Hitler became increasingly confident. He openly began to overthrow the Treaty of Versailles.

What Hitler wanted – steps to war

1 In 1936 Hitler remilitarized the Rhinelands (he sent German soldiers to occupy the area).

2 In 1938 Hitler took over Austria.

3 Also in 1938 he took over part of Czechoslavakia.

4 In March 1939 he took over Bohemia.

5 In September 1939 Hitler attacked Poland. At this point Britain and France declared war on Germany.

Source C

1933	1.9	1938	18.4
1936	5.8	1939	32.3

▲ Money spent by the German government on the army and armaments in billions of marks.

Source D

Number of battalions in:

	1933	1936	1939
Infantry	84	334	906
Artillery	24	148	482
Tank	0	16	34

▲ The increase in the size of the German army, 1933–9.

QUESTIONS

1 Read **Blitzkrieg**

   a What does Blitzkreig mean?

   b Write three sentences on what Hitler said the German army would do.

HERMANN GOERING 1893–1946

Goering was a great fighter pilot in the First World War. He joined the Nazi Party in the 1920s and joined Hitler's government in 1933. He was the man who in 1933 persuaded President Hindenburg to use his emergency powers to weaken opposition to the Nazis in the elections to the Reichstag. As Prime Minister of Prussia he set up the Gestapo and the first concentration camps. He also ignored the Treaty of Versailles and set up the Luftwaffe (German airforce). He was in charge of Hitler's **Four Year Plan** (1936–1940) and was made Reichsmarshal by Hitler in 1940.

However, during the Second World War Hitler blamed Goering for the Luftwaffe's failure to defeat Britain. In 1945 Goering was captured by the Allies and condemned to death at the Nuremberg trials. He committed suicide on the night before his execution.

1 Read Source 2. Why do you think the Nazis stopped persecuting the Jews during the Olympic Games?

2 Study Sources 4 and 5.
  a What was Jesse Owens' achievement at the Berlin Olympics?
  b Hitler refused to shake hands with Owens. How can this be explained?
  c What might the spectators have thought about Hitler's behaviour?

3 Study Source 1 and re-read pages 50–51. Why would Hitler have been keen to stage the Olympic Games in Berlin?

4 Source 2 says the Germans were happy and united under Hitler in 1936. Do you agree with this view?
(Pages 48–9 and page 54 will help.)

▶ An official poster for the Olympic Games held in Berlin, 1936.

Source 2

The Olympic Games were held in Berlin in August 1936. The signs 'Jews not welcome' were quietly taken down from shops and hotels, the persecution of the Jews halted for a time and the country put on its best behaviour. No earlier games had seen such organization, nor such a lavish display of entertainment. The visitors, especially those from England and America, were greatly impressed by what they saw – a happy, friendly people united under Hitler.

▲ From a history of Nazi Germany written in the USA in 1959.

Source 3

The people's state must organize its educational work in such a way that the bodies of the young are trained from infancy onwards, so as to be tempered and hardened for the demands made on them in later years. Not a day should be allowed in which the young pupil does not have one hour of physical training in the morning and one in the evening.

▲ Hitler wrote down his views about the importance of physical education in *Mein Kampf*, first published in 1925.

Source 4

▲ The famous black athlete, Jesse Owens of the USA, winning the men's 100 metres final at the Berlin Olympics. He won three individual gold medals and one team gold (for the 4 by 100 metres relay).

Source 5

The athletic events of the Olympic Games at Berlin ended on August 9. By then most of the Olympic records had been beaten and a number of new world records had been set up. There was no doubt that Jesse Owens, the American negro, had put up the most wonderful of many performances. Others of America's negro team, notably Metcalfe and Woodruff, also covered themselves with glory.

▲ A report from the *Illustrated London News*, August 1936.

CHAPTER 4

LIFE IN THE THIRD REICH

4.1 Did the people benefit from Nazi economic policies?

When the Nazis came to power in 1933, they promised that everyone would be better off. Did this actually happen? This section looks at some of the evidence which may help us decide.

Fewer people unemployed

Look at Source B. After 1933 there were fewer and fewer people unemployed. So the Nazis had created more jobs throughout the country.

But…

Fewer and fewer people were unemployed in other countries as well after 1933 (including Britain and the USA). The world was coming out of the Depression. It was not necessarily the Nazi government that was responsible for lower employment.

Wages rising

Look at Source C. By 1934 wages were starting to go up again after the worst years of the Great Depression.

But…

Wages were still lower in 1938 than they had been in 1928. However, Source D shows that Germany's national income (all the money Germany earned) was higher in 1938 than in 1928. It looks as if the German people were not sharing in the growing national income.

Putting more in than they were getting out

In 1939 German workers were working about four hours a week more than they had been in 1928. And they were earning less money than in 1928 (see Source C and Source E on page 64).

Source A

No one would say that the German standard of living is a high one, but it has been rising in recent years.

▲ Written in 1938 by a visitor to Germany.

Source B

Unemployed in Germany (in millions)

Year	Value	Year	Value
1928	1.8	1935	2.2
1932	6.0	1936	1.6
1933	4.8	1937	0.9
1934	2.7	1938	0.5

Source C

Index of wages

Year	Value	Year	Value
1928	125	1936	100
1933	88	1938	106
1934	94		

▲ The term 'index' means that the wages in one year, in this case 1936, are taken to be 100. The other years are measured against this.

Source D

National income
(in billions of marks)

1928	72	1936	64
1932	43	1938	80
1933	44		

Source E

Wages as a percentage of national income

1928	62	1934	62
1932	64	1936	59
1933	63	1938	57

Source F

The workers compared their lives under the Third Reich with the bad times of 1932, not with the better and more representative times of 1929. By giving the workers a little more the Nazis appeared to be improving things drastically, even though the standard of living was below that of the late 1920s.

▲ Adapted from Richard Grunberger, *A Social History of the Third Reich*, 1971.

Source G

Index of industrial and consumer goods

Industrial		Consumer
100	1928	100
56	1933	80
81	1934	91
114	1936	100
144	1938	116

Where was the extra money going?

If the national income had gone up but the workers were earning a smaller part of it, where was the extra money going? The answer was war goods. The Nazi government wanted to prepare for war so it needed to make tanks, guns, aeroplanes and machinery. Money was spent setting up factories to make these things and other sorts of machinery (industrial goods).

Industrial goods and consumer goods

Industrial goods were important to the Nazis because they were useful for war. Consumer goods were interesting to ordinary people because they were things like cars, radios and bicycles. The Nazis did not want the German people to have too many consumer goods in the shops. If there was less to spend their money on, the ordinary people would feel better off. In Source G industrial goods and consumer goods are indexed at the same level (100) in 1928. We can then see that the workforce in Nazi Germany produced industrial goods much faster than consumer goods.

Did the German people get other benefits?

The Nazis set up two organizations to care directly for the workers' interests.

1 The Beauty of Labour (SDA). This aimed to improve cleanliness, lighting and noise levels at work. It also provided hot meals in the workplace. These benefits were meant to take the place of higher wages.

2 The Strength through Joy (KDF) movement aimed to fill the workers' spare time with sports, camping and leisure activities. The best workers might qualify for a cruise on a KDF liner (see Source H).

Nazi propaganda

The Nazi Party propaganda was run by Joseph Goebbels. He used every sort of propaganda. He used the radio, films, newspapers and rumours or whispering campaigns. He made sure that the German workers heard what the Nazis wanted them to hear whether it was true or not. For instance, they were told that workers in the Soviet Union and Britain were worse off than German workers. This was true about the Soviet Union but not true about Britain.

Better or worse than trade unions?

A trade union is a workers' organization. It is there to bargain with employers over wages and hours of work for the workers.

The Beauty of Labour and the Strength through Joy were not trade unions. They did not bargain with employers over wages and hours of work. They did not protect workers, who had no one to put their point of view.

Some workers realized that the government was making use of them to meet its own ends – to prepare for war as quickly as possible. Their wages did not go up, their working hours increased, and it was impossible for them to say anything. Nor did they have time to think as they had to pursue the activities out of working hours dictated by the KDF.

▶ A few of the leisure activities organized by Strength through Joy (KDF).

Source H

Die Deutsche Arbeitsfront

Urlauberfahrten zur See

N. S.-Gemeinschaft »Kraft durch Freude«

▲ A Strength through Joy (KDF) poster of 1938, advertising cruises for the German workforce.

Source I

Concerts, operas, theatre, films, gymnastics, swimming, boxing, wrestling, water sports, winter sports, factory sports, cruises, hikes.

Source J

A 1938 poster promoting the *Volkswagen*, or people's car. It tells people to save five marks per week to buy their own car.

Source K

REICHSAUTOBAHNEN IN DEUTSCHLAND

A poster advertising the German autobahns.

New cars and new roads

The Nazis developed a new car. People could aim to save enough money to own one. It was called the *Volkswagen* or 'people's car'. The Nazis also promised new, fast roads, called autobahns.

However, most people could not save enough money to buy one of these cars. And also there were never enough made. Germany made less than half the cars Britain did in the 1930s, although Britain was a smaller country. The good roads were mostly built in preparation for war time so that soldiers and tanks could move around quickly.

QUESTIONS

1 Read page 64. Write a few lines about:

 • The Beauty of Labour
 • Strength through Joy

2 Read page 65. Were the workers better off under the Nazis? Explain your answer.

ducation

/ith parents at home. A child first arns at home. Even in 1933 many eople did not vote for Hitler, so many hildren would not have heard much bout him (in a positive way) at home.

t school. Things were very different at chool. Every subject was used to put orward Nazi ideas (see Source D). he Nazis knew what sort of people they anted. They wanted soldiers. So boys ere taught military skills. They wanted ood mothers of healthy soldiers. So girls ere taught about looking after the home nd family.

Did children like school under the Nazis?

There was more time for sport and less for studying books. Some children liked this. Some did not. Some girls felt cheated that they had to spend more time learning cooking and domestic skills. Some liked it better than studying books.

Source **B**

The whole purpose of education is to create Nazis.

▲ Said by the Nazi Minister of Education, Bernhard Rust.

Source **C**

German language, History, Geography, Chemistry and Mathematics must teach ...the glory of military service and of German heroes.

▲ From a Nazi statement on the purpose of education for boys.

Source **D**

To build a lunatic asylum costs 6 million marks. How many houses at 15,000 marks each could be built for that?

▲ A problem from a Mathematics textbook in the late 1930s, showing how even Mathematics was used to teach Nazi ideas about killing the insane.

Source **A**

◀ Hitler shown with children.

Source E

◄ Photograph of a Hitler Youth camp in 1934, showing how big such camps were.

For active children the Nazis provided plenty to do outside school. And this was often fun.

The Hitler Youth – Boys

By 1936 everyone had to belong to the Hitler Youth at one level or another.

1 Pimpf (Little Fellows) was for boys from 6-10 years old. There was plenty of camping and games.

2 Deutsch Jungvolk was for boys from 10-14 years old. As well as camping, walking and so on, the boys learnt about Nazi ideas and about the army.

3 Hitler Jugend (Hitler Youth) was for boys from 14-18 years old. A lot of time was spent on army training.

The Hitler Youth – Girls

Up to the age of 14 years, girls joined the **Jungmädel** (Young Maidens). They were taught to care for their health and get ready to look after a family.

Girls aged 14-21 joined the **League of German Maidens**. There were healthy activities (see Source H) and more learning about looking after a family.

Source F

▲ A fund-raising poster for the Hitler Youth.

Source G

Year	Number of 10–18 year-olds in Hitler Youth (boys and girls)	Total number of 10–18 year-olds in the population
1933	2.3	7.5
1934	3.6	7.7
1935	3.9	8.2
1936	5.4	8.7
1937	5.9	9.1
1938	7.0	9.1
1939	7.3	8.9

▲ Membership of the Hitler Youth, 1933–9 (figures in millions).

Source H

We had to go to meetings, youth rallies and sports. The weekends were crammed with outings, campings and marches. It was all fun in a way and good exercise but we had no time for schoolwork.

▶ A. Klonne, *Youth in the Third Reich*, 1982.

◀ A description of the League of German Maidens, by a former member.

How popular was the Hitler Youth?

There are many photographs of Hitler with children (see Source A on page 67). He was particularly keen to identify with youth and show his popularity with young people.

It is difficult to tell how popular the Hitler Youth was. We have two sources of evidence. One is Nazi propaganda with films like *Triumph of the Will* (see page 59), photographs (Source E) and posters (Source F). These all show it to be great fun and also show the huge numbers involved.

The second is the what the young people thought (often when they looked back years later). Sources H and I give a mixed impression of the Hitler Youth.

Other youth groups

The Nazis killed off other youth groups as far as they could. But new ones sprang up. Many of these went against the Nazis. Sometimes these groups deliberately dressed or did things in ways the Nazis did not like (see Sources J and K).

Gangs

Some groups went even further. They were really gangs. The most well known was the **Eidelweiss Pirates**.

Source I

When I became a leader in the Jungvolk ...I found the requirement of absolute obedience unpleasant...I saw there must be discipline in such a large group of boys, but it was exaggerated.

Source J

▲ Two 'swing types' from a book on youth criminality, published in Germany in 1941.

Source K

▲ An 'English casual' from the same book as above.

Source L

◄ Edelweiss Pirates being publicl[y] hanged in Cologne in 1944.

Source M

Every child knows who the Kittelbach Pirates are. Ther[e] are more of them than ther[e] are Hitler Youth...They're always down by the canal.

▲ The complaint of a mining instructor from Oberhausen, 194[ ]

Two other gangs were the **Kittelbach Pirates** (Source M) and the **Navajos Gang** (Source N).

What did the gangs do?

Some of the gangs beat up Hitler Youth groups. During the Second World War some helped Allied airmen who had been shot down over Germany. If the Gestapo caught them they were hanged.

Source N

▲ Members of the Navajos, a Cologne based gang,1940.

Conclusion

The Nazis did wipe out most of the other youth groups. They made the Hitler Youth fun and exciting and probably many young people enjoyed the camping and leisure activities. But if you were not for the Nazis you were against them. There was no middle way. Some young people did not like what they saw of the Nazi way of life. They formed gangs to work against Hitler and the Nazis. By the end there were more rebellious gangs under the Nazi régime than there were during the Weimar Republic.

QUESTIONS

1 Read page 68 and **Education** on page 67.

a What activities were provided in the Hitler Youth?

b What was the purpose of these activities?

The Nazi view of women

A woman's job was to have children and look after her husband and family (see Source A). Women had a different role to men. There was no question of equality under the Nazis. Women were squeezed out of jobs soon after Hitler came to power. Women doctors and civil servants were the first to go. Women teachers were not appointed. Women were not allowed to be judges or lawers, as they were considered 'too emotional'.

What did women think?

Some women had always believed that looking after a husband and children was their only job. Some may have been converted to the Nazi ideas. Other women probably kept quiet because they found it easier or were afraid. Some women, however, did protest.

How did women protest?

Some women joined the Social Democrats or the Communists. Many women supported the Nazis but protested about the Nazi view of women. They said that being a mother did not suit every woman and some women had special talents for certain jobs.

How paid work for women

The Nazis did not pay attention to women's protests. On the other hand as more and more men went into the army in the Second World War, women were needed as factory workers.

Source A

Unterstützt das hilfswerk
Mutter und Kind

▲ A Nazi propaganda poster showing how the Nazis saw the role of women.

Source B

The female bird preens herself for her mate and hatches her eggs for him. Women have the same task.

▲ Goebbels' view of the role of women.

Source C

Equal rights for women means they are valued for the job nature has given them.

▲ Hitler's view on 'equality' for women.

The Nazis soon stopped talking about women staying at home. They said it was women's duty to support Germany and go to work in factories and on farms. But, they were paid less than men and were given the lowest jobs.

Why were the Nazis so keen on family life?

There were two reasons why the Nazis were keen on family life.

First it was at home, in the family, that children first learnt what to think. If they were brought up in a good Nazi family, they would be good Nazis themselves (see Source G).

Second, if women stayed at home they could concentrate on having babies. This would mean a bigger and bigger German population for fighting and conquering new land.

How did the Nazis encourage large families?

1 They banned birth control and abortion.

2 They gave marriage loans and family allowances.

3 They gave medals to women who had many children.

4 They encouraged childless couples to divorce so that each partner would find someone else.

Source D

We see our daughters growing up in stupid aimlessness, living only in the vain hope of perhaps getting a man and having children.

▲ German women to Adolf Hitler, 1934.

Source E

Not only have women teachers a right to their own existence, but bringing up children needs the best training of mothers.

▲ Head of the women's section of the Nazi Teachers Organization.

Source F

Women doctors could aid mothers. Women teachers would be best for teaching young girls. Women jurists would be best at dealing with cases about children.

▲ The view of a Nazi feminist in 1937.

Rules for the purity of race

At the same time the Nazis made rules to protect the purity of the race. No one was allowed to marry a Jew. Anyone who had an inherited illness, such as blindness or epilepsy, had to be sterilized.

Source G

A Nazi official and his family.

Source H

One of the worst effects of the Nazi Youth movement is that our children no longer get any peace. I dread to think the kind of people they will grow up into if they have this propaganda thundering at them all the time.

How a German mother felt about the Hitler Youth. From E. Amy Buller, *Darkness over Germany*, 1945.

QUESTIONS

1 Look at Source A on page 71 and Source G above. What do they say is the main job of women?

2 Read **Why were the Nazis so keen on family life?** on page 72.

   Why did the Nazis want women to stay at home?

3 Read Sources D, E and F on page 72. Did all women agree with the Nazis that they should stay at home?

What is a minority?

In most countries there is a majority. Most people living in China are Chinese. But there is a small number of British people who live there. They are a minority. There are other minorities too. If most people are heterosexual, then homosexuals are a minority. Most people live in a set place. They are the majority. If people travel around like gypsies and tramps they are in the minority.

In a democracy a person has a right to belong to a minority. In Nazi Germany there were no such rights. The Nazis did not want minorities. They wanted only pure German people (Aryans).

Who were the minorities in Nazi Germany?

The Jews, gypsies, insane people, tramps, beggers and alcoholics were minorities that the Nazis did not want.

- **Jews**. The Jews were the main target. They were persecuted throughout the 1930s.

  By the time of the Second World War most Jews must have known that they had no rights left at all. Many thought they might be forced to move out of Germany. They did not know they might be put in death camps (see pages 83-6).

- **Gypsies**. These were travelling people. The Nazis disliked them for two reasons. They were not pure Germans. They did not work in a set place. The Nazis dealt with them in

Source A

The extermination of the Jews has had most attention. But although understandable, it has led people to overlook the fact that there was a broad campaign against many groups who were considered to be 'alien to the community'.

▲ From an article by Jeremy Noakes in *History Today* 1985.

Source B

The gypsy question can only be solved when most have been put in camps and made to work and when this half-breed population has finally been prevented from having children.

▲ From a comment by Robert Ritter, a Nazi expert on how gypsies should be treated.

two ways. They made gypsies live in one place. Then they sterilized them. Eventually most gypsies were killed.

- **Insane people**. Those who were mentally ill were no use to the Nazis. At first they were sterilized. Later many died by means of 'mercy killing' with injections or gas.

Tramps and beggars. Like the gypsies, tramps and beggars had no fixed home and no fixed work. They did not fit in with Nazi ideas. From 1933 tramps and beggars were rounded up and put in forced labour camps. Many were sterilized in case they 'polluted' German women.

Homosexuals. These were despised by the Nazis because this was not what a German hero should be. Yet many Nazis, particularly in the SA, were homosexuals themselves. This was ignored. But other homosexuals were put in concentration camps and often sterilized.

Alcoholics. Heavy drinking was discouraged. Alcoholics could be rounded up and have their heads shaved. Some were sent to concentration camps.

What happened to the minorities?

is very unlikely that any of the Jews oresaw what was to come. They did not oresee that they might be put in death amps.

Source C

In the case of community aliens [minorities] who are burdens, welfare help is not needed. They must be forced to work or prevented from being a further burden.

▲ A police order, 1940.

QUESTIONS

1 Why did the Nazis dislike the gypsies?

2 Why did the Nazis dislike tramps and beggars?

3 Why did the Nazis dislike homosexuals?

4 The Nazis sometimes talked about the 'final solution'. By reading what happened to the minorities work out what the 'final solution' meant. Write one sentence to explain it.

.5 What did the German people think of Hitler?

he Nazi Party was not always popular Germany. But Hitler, himself, was ery popular (see Source A). He was rusted by the old and idolized by the oung.

he reasons for Hitler's popularity have een much talked about, but there are wo main ones: first the German people elt the need of a strong leader, second, litler's own image.

Source A

It is true that criticism of the [German] Government is forbidden. Yet I have heard the speeches of Nazi speakers freely condemned.
But not a word of criticism or of disapproval have I heard of Hitler.

▲ From an article by David Lloyd George, former British Prime Minister, in the *Daily Express*, 1936.

The history of Germany

There had often been very strong leaders in Germany. One of these was **Frederick the Great** (1740–1788). Then all the German states united in 1871 under the strong leadership of **Bismarck**. This new Germany was ruled by a **Kaiser** (Emperor). Hitler saw himself as the next strong leader.

How did Hitler show himself to be a strong leader?

Hitler was brilliant at public speaking. His speeches were dramatic. They captured the attention of the audience. Hitler said he would lead all Germans. He would make Germany great and rich and end the Treaty of Versailles. He had portraits painted showing him as strong and confident (Source D).

Why did the Germans accept Hitler?

Many people suffered from the Depression in 1929. Businesses collapsed. People lost their jobs. They lost their savings.

Source B

For ten years after 1933 Hitler was very popular. We need to look at Hitler's image, how the German people saw their leader: the 'Hitler myth'.

They saw their leader in two ways. One was the image built up by all the new techniques of propaganda. The other image was of the 'Superman' political leader which was traditional and acceptable to the German people.

▲ Adapted from an article by Ian Kershaw, in *History Today*.

Source C

► Hitler speaking in 1933.

Source D

▲ A portrait of Hitler, painted by Heinrich Knirr, 1937.

Source E

▲ Hitler idolized by crowds.

▼ Hitler idolized by youth.

Source F

There were so many parties in the Reichstag that they could not agree on what to do to help the German people. So the German people did not know where to turn. Hitler told them that he would solve their problems.

How did Hitler tell people?

Hitler spoke at huge meetings and on the radio so everyone in Germany knew his voice. He developed very effective techniques to excite listeners in his favour.

1 What sorts of books were burnt by the Nazis? (See Sources 2 and 4.)

2 Look at Source 1 and re-read page 67. Why did the Nazis encourage young people to burn books?

3 Did the writer of Source 2 agree with the book-burning? Explain your answer.

Source 1

▲ Hitler Youth helping to burn books and pictures in Salzburg in 1938.

Source 2

The 'shame' of which my father spoke was the Nazis' book-burning, which Dr Barsch had chosen to describe as a glorius occasion. On the evening of 10 May, book-burnings had taken place in front of the Humboldt University in Berlin and in many other university towns. The works of all Jewish authors were tossed into flames, as were the writings of others who for one reason or another were hated by the Nazis. The list of nearly twenty thousand writers included almost every important name in German letters [literature].

▲ A description by Bernt Engelmann, a German anti-Nazi resistance worker. Dr Barsch was a former family friend who worked for a newspaper. He claimed he was forced to write an article praising the book-burnings. From *In Hitler's Germany*, published in 1986.

Source 3

The soul of the German people can again express itself. These flames do not only cast light on the end of an old era. They also light up the new one.

▲ Dr Joseph Goebbels, speaking at a bonfire of books in Berlin on 10 May 1933. Over 20,000 books were burned, including many by Germany's most famous authors.

Source 4

A huge bonfire of books judged by the Nazis to be 'un-German' is burning tonight in the square in front of Berlin University. A similar bonfire burnt in Munich where thousands of school children watched… 'As you watch the fire burn these un-German books', the children were told, 'let it also burn into your hearts love of the Fatherland'… New books ordered by the libraries are to be by writers unknown abroad and, from their titles, seem to be novels written to glorify war.

▲ A report by an English newspaper about the book burning in Germany in May 1933.

CHAPTER 5

THE IMPACT OF WAR ON THE THIRD REICH

5.1 Hitler's attitude to war

What is war for?

War is a way of getting what the politicians want if they cannot get it by bargaining. In most cases a country and its politicians want more land. Usually war is the last resort and for most people war is an exceptional period, an emergency. When a country has got more land (or been defeated in war and not got more land), the war stops.

Hitler's attitude to war

Hitler believed four things:
1. That struggle is natural to human life.
2. That the highest form of struggle is war.
3. That a master race like the Germans would want more land.
4. That the obvious lands for the Germans to occupy were Poland and the Soviet Union to the east.

Hitler therefore turned the usual attitude to war inside out. Instead of being the exception, war was to become a normal state. Sources B to E show Hitler's ideas.

Source A

War is the continuation of policy [getting what you want] by other means.

▲ From *On War* by Karl von Clausewitz (1780–1831).

Source B

All of nature is one struggle between strength and weakness, an eternal victory of the strong over the weak.

▲ From a speech by Hitler in 1923.

Source C

War is the most natural, the most ordinary thing...War is life. All struggle is war.

▲ Adolf Hitler, *Mein Kampf*, 1925.

Source D

We turn our eyes to the land in the East.

▲ Adolf Hitler, *Mein Kampf*, 1925.

Source E

According to an eternal law of Nature, the right to land belongs to the one who conquers the land because there was not enough space for the growth of the population.

▲ Adapted from Hitler's *Second Book*, 1928.

The Second World War fell into two parts for the Germans. During the first part Germany did well and civilian life was not affected. During the second part Germany did badly and people at home suffered.

The first part – 1939–1941

This was the time of **Blitzkrieg** which means 'lightning war'. The German armies swept into country after country – like lightning. They conquered Poland, Denmark, Norway, Holland, Belgium and Luxembourg and then France. They could not be stopped. The German people were delighted. They were successful and lovely things poured into Germany from the conquered countries. Everything from gold and paintings to silk stockings and perfume. Hitler was very popular.

The second part – 1941–45

This was the time of **total war**. By 1941 Hitler had conquered a great deal of land. Now he had to hold it. This used many soldiers. Moreover, Hitler had not defeated Britain and Britain had chosen to go on fighting. Hitler turned his attention to the **Soviet Union**. In the summer of 1941 he sent a huge army to invade the Soviet Union. At first the army was successful. Then the Soviet Union stopped the Germans and slowly began to drive them back.

Hardship for the Germans

By 1942 the good times were over. The German people had to work harder and harder to pay for the army, the guns, the aeroplanes and the tanks. Food was rationed. Many families lost sons, husbands and fathers fighting the Soviet Union.

Source **A**

▲ The weapons of *Blitzkrieg*.

Source **B**

The nation is filled with a trust in the Führer such as has never before existed to this extent.

▲ A district leader, 1940.

Source **C**

German farmers will live in beautiful settlements [in eastern Europe]. The [German] governors will have palaces.

▶ From *Hitler's Table Talk*, 1942.

Goebbels and Total War – 1943

The German Government conducted a propaganda campaign to raise morale. Joseph Goebbels was head of the German Ministry of Propaganda. Even before the war the Ministry's budget was 55.3 million Reichsmarks. By 1943 the Ministry was pouring out propaganda. Special announcements were made on the radio about German victories (true or untrue). The announcements were made with great fanfares of music.

Meanwhile Goebbels wrote newspaper articles and made speeches. He made one very brilliant speech in 1943. He inspired the German people to go on working and fighting so that they could have total victory (see Sources F and G).

Source D

	Germany	USSR
Tanks	9,300	24,700
Aircraft	14,700	25,400
Artillery	12,000	127,000

▲ German and Soviet arms production, 1942.

Source F

I ask you: Do you believe with the Führer and with us in the final total victory of the German people? I ask you: Are you determined to follow the Führer through thick and thin in the struggle for victory and to put up even with the heaviest personal burdens?
I ask you: Do you want total war?

▲ From Goebbels' speech on total war in the Berlin Sports Palace, 1943.

Source E

DER SIEG WIRD UNSER SEIN!

▲ A Nazi propaganda poster of 1942: 'Victory will be ours!'

Source G

▲ A photograph of the audience listening to Goebbels' speech in the Berlin Sports Palace, 1943.

The bombing of German cities – 1943–44

From 1943 the Allies started to bomb German cities. Thousands and thousands of Germans were killed in the bombing of cities such as Cologne, Hamburg, Dresden and Berlin. The bombing did not break the Germans' will to win. But the bombing and the losses of soldiers fighting the Soviet Union made it more and more obvious that Germany was not winning the war. Soon some Germans began to doubt Hitler.

Source H

Many German cities were devastated. Perhaps the outstanding example was Hamburg, where a series of attacks in July and August of 1943 destroyed 55 to 60 per cent of the city. 12.5 square miles were completely burned out and 75,000 people made homeless. German estimates range from 60,000 to 100,000 persons killed, many of them in shelters where they were reached by carbon-monoxide poisoning.

Of the total destruction, 75-80 per cent was due to fires, particularly to those so-called fire storms.

▲ Report from the US strategic bombing survey, September 1945.

Source I

▲ The destruction of Dresden by Allied bombing, February 1945.

QUESTIONS

1 Read page 80. Write a few lines about.

 • Blitzkreig 1939–41
 • Total war 1941–45

2 Read **Hardship for the Germans** on page 80 and look at Source I. In what ways did the German people at home suffer?

3 Read page 81. How did the Nazis try to keep people's spirits up?

Treatment of the Jews before the war

In the 1930s the Jews in Germany suffered occasional outbreaks of organized violence such as Crystal Night (page 55). From the beginning of the war in 1939, however, the persecution of the Jews increased greatly. From 1941, the Nazis came up with the '**Final Solution**'.

Extermination camps

There were many concentration (forced labour) camps in Germany in the 1930s. From 1941 extermination camps were built too (see map below). These were mainly in Poland. Six million Jews were murdered in these camps between 1941 and 1945.

Did Hitler always mean to kill the Jews?

Historians have argued about this. Some say Hitler always meant to kill the Jews (Source A). Hitler wrote his ideas about the Jews in his book, *Mein Kampf*. These ideas led directly to the **genocide** (mass killing) of the Jews. Others say he probably meant just to expel them from Germany. It was the war that changed his mind (Source B).

Source A

Race dogma was vitally important to Hitler.

▲ Adapted from K. Hildebrand, a German historian.

Source B

The killing of the Jews came about not only because it was intended to destroy them but also because the Nazi régime had reached a point of no return.

▲ Adapted from M. Broszat, a German historian.

- The main concentration camps.
- ◉ The main extermination camps.
- ▨ The Third Reich

◀ Nazi concentration and extermination camps in Germany and in German-occupied countries.

Source C

I was ordered ... to set up the extermination building at Auschwitz. I used Cyclon B, which was a crystallised prussic acid. We dropped it into the death chamber through a small hole. It took from three to fifteen minutes to kill everyone, depending on the weather.

We knew when people were dead because their screaming stopped. We waited half an hour before opening the doors. Our special squads took off the gold rings and took out the gold-filled teeth from the dead bodies.

▲ A description of methods of killing the Jews at Auschwitz by Rudolf Hoess.

How did war affect Hitler's ideas on killing the Jews?

War certainly speeded up Hitler's persecution of the Jews in four main ways:

1 Hitler was too busy fighting a war to move all the millions of Jews far away from Germany.
2 Germany conquered Poland and other land in the east. There were many Jews living in Poland and the other eastern countries. They presented Hitler with a new problem.
3 The German soldiers and the SS came across these Jews. They wanted to know how to treat them. The SS were told to kill them. Many soldiers in the German army were unhappy about this.
4 All the Germans were busy fighting the war. It was easier for Hitler to keep his killing of the Jews secret from most people during the wartime emergency than during peace .

The Holocaust

The mass-murder of the Jews has become known as the **Holocaust**. The Nazis used two means of mass murder in Poland and eastern Europe.

Source D

► The remains of ovens at Auschwitz, which were used to cremate the bodies of people killed in the gas chambers. This photograph was taken in 1995.

- The SS shot Jews with machine guns.

- The Nazis set up extermination camps where the Jews were killed in gas chambers. In Auschwitz camp alone, two million Jews were killed.

Mass killing and medical experiments at Auschwitz

Rudolf Hoess, the commandant at Auschwitz, described the way the gassing was done (Source C). Then the bodies were burnt in ovens that were made in ordinary German factories (see Source D).

At the same time some German doctors took the opportunity to do experiments on Jewish prisoners who could not, of course, protest. One of the doctors was called Josef Mengele. He often carried out experiments or operations without using anaesthetics.

Should we forget the Holocaust?

Many people say we should never forget the Holocaust. It was the worst mass killing ever known – and sadly there have been many others too in history.

Other people say we should forget it. Among these was Heinrich Himmler, the SS leader who felt the extermination of the Jews should always be kept secret (Source F).

After the war many Nazi leaders said it had not happened at all. Some historians have said it was no worse than the Allies (Americans and British) bombing Dresden in the war and killing thousands of people.

Source E

I have never accepted that Mengele believed he was doing serious medical work.... He was exercising power.
Major surgery was performed without anaesthetic. Once I witnessed a stomach operation – Mengele was removing pieces from the stomach, but without any anaesthesia. It was horrifying.

▲ The memories of Alex Dekel, a Romanian Jew who was himself experimented on at Auschwitz. Dekel published a book about his experiences in 1941.

Source F

Among ourselves we can talk openly about it, though we will never speak a word in public... I am speaking about the evacuation of the Jews, the extermination of the Jewish people..That is a page of glory in our history that ...never will be written.

▲ Himmler speaking to a meeting of SS officers in 1943.

Anne Frank and Rudolf Hoess

These two people were both famous after the war for very different reasons. Anne Frank was an innocent victim of the persecution by the Nazis. Rudolf Hoess was one of the organizers of the persecution.

ANNE FRANK (1929–45)

Anne Frank was a Jewish girl born in Germany. Her family fled to Holland. When the Nazis took over Holland they went into hiding in Amsterdam. They stayed there for two years until they were betrayed and sent to different concentration camps. Anne died in Bergen-Belsen in March 1945, aged 16 and only weeks before the end of the war. She is remembered through her diary which she kept throughout her period in hiding. Her father found it and published it after the war.

Source G, which is an extract from this diary, shows how hurt the Jewish people were at being singled out for persecution.

RUDOLF HOESS (1900–47)

Hoess was a leading member of the SS. He became commandant of Auschwitz extermination camp in 1940. He was responsible for the gassing and shooting of over 2.5 million people. He was captured after the war and brought to trial. He was executed in 1947.

During his trial a great deal of information came out about conditions at Auschwitz and the experiments of Mengele. Hoess always claimed he was a normal man, acting on orders.

Source G

Our many Jewish friends are being taken away...They are treated by the Gestapo without a shred of decency...It is impossible to escape; most of the people in the camp are branded as inmates by their shaven heads... If it as bad as this in Holland what will it be like where they are sent to?

▲ From the *Diary of Anne Frank*, 9 October 1942, describing life for Jews outside the Frank's hiding place.

Source H

I am completely normal. Even while I was carrying out the job of extermination I led a normal family life... I have always seen and felt for human suffering... From our training the thought of refusing an order just didn't enter one's head.

▲ Rudolf Hoess describing himself.

QUESTIONS

1 Read pages 83 and 84.

   a Did Hitler want to kill the Jews from the beginning?

   b How much did war affect Hitler's ideas on the Jews?

2 Look at all the sources on pages 84–6. Do you think we should remember the Holocaust? Give reasons for your answer.

Life in the Ghetto of Lodz

This section is a study of the life of a Jewish community during the Holocaust.

The Germans invade Poland, September 1939

Over three million Jews lived in Poland. Many lived together in the cities. The Nazis made the Jewish areas within a city into closed-off ghettoes. The Jews could not leave the ghettoes which were surrounded by walls and barbed wire.

The Ghetto of Lodz

The ghetto of the city of Lodz is shown in the map. At first the Germans sent Jews from Germany and Austria to Lodz. It became overcrowded.

Then as the war continued the Jews were taken out of the ghetto and put on trains for Auschwitz and Chelmo, the two death camps not far away. By the end of 1944, the ghetto was empty.

Work in the ghetto

The Germans used Jews to work in factories and workshops in the ghettoes. They made things like clothes. Some worked as road menders and builders outside the ghetto. The Jewish people were allowed to run the ghetto themselves and tried to make the German rules less harsh (see Sources A and B). Children, too, were put to work in the workshops. And again the Jewish people tried to help them by setting up classes in secret so the children could have some education.

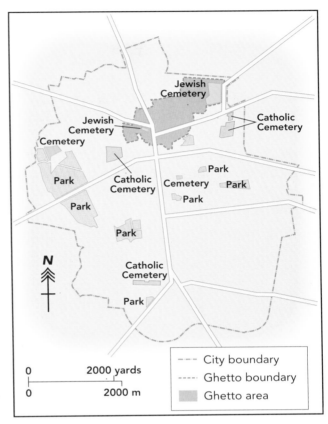

▲ The city of Lodz in 1939 showing the ghetto area.

Source A

Some men hide from being forced to work outside the ghetto. They are fearful too of being sent away from the ghetto. They draw no rations because their food cards have been cancelled. So have those of their families.

▲ Adapted from the *Chronicle of the Ghetto of Lodz*, Monday 21 February 1944.

How do we know?

We know a great deal about what it was like to live in the ghetto of Lodz. This is because a number of people wrote a secret diary or *Chronicle* between 1941 and 1944.

The *Chronicle of the Ghetto of Lodz*

The *Chronicle* was written very carefully. The writers did not say anything against the Germans. They wrote about everyday things in the ghetto. They wrote about how to cook frozen and rotten potatoes. They wrote about work, about births, deaths and suicide and about people being deported.

Source C

With a helpless look the girl scans the room.
The pranks of the naughty dwarfs
Always wrecking her stitches.

Source B

There were about 40 children. The room was small and there was constant fear of a surprise German inspection and fear that informers would tell the Germans about the teaching. Whenever a German team came into the factory, the children would instantly turn the room into a work area.

▲ From Sara Grober, *Jewish Public Activities in the Lodz Ghetto*, 1979.

QUESTIONS

1 Read page 87. Write a few lines about life for the Jews in the Ghetto of Lodz.

2 Read **The *Chronicle of the Ghetto of Lodz***. Why do you think people in the ghetto wanted to write a diary or chronicle of what happened day by day?

Source D

Dawn...
The sun with golden glow lights up the mountain peak and then just a minute later
Heads of flowers peek from the blades of grass
And see a castle, as in legends.

▲ Pictures and verse produced in the Lodz Ghetto.

Before the war and the first part of the war

Some people spoke against Hitler before the war. But when Germany was first at war and doing well, few people spoke out.

The second part of the war – total war

After 1941 more people spoke out against Hitler. This opposition was called **resistance**.

Student resistance

Some students formed the **White Rose** group, appealing for passive resistance to the Nazis. Leaflets were issued telling people not to co-operate with the Party.

Conservative resistance

Some people had supported Hitler but now felt he was going too far. They wanted to overthrow him before it was too late. One of the leaders was **Ulrich von Hassell**. Another was **Carl Goerdeler**.

Christian resistance

Many Christians – both Catholic and Protestant – spoke out against Nazi ideas.

Army resistance

Some officers like **General Beck** had already tried to oppose Hitler before the war. After 1941, famous soldiers like **Field Marshal Rommel** and **Admiral Canaris** opposed him. The most famous attempt to remove Hitler was the bomb placed by Count von Stauffenberg in Hitler's headquarters in July 1944. Hitler escaped with slight wounds. Everyone who had anything to do with the bomb was hanged. The statements in Source C (page 90) would have been broadcast in newspapers and on the radio if Hitler had been killed.

Source A

In the name of German youth, we demand from Adolf Hitler's state the restoration of personal freedom, which it took from us by deceit.

There can be but one word of action for us: Fight the party! Quit the party organizations, where all discussion is being stifled.

▲ From a student pamphlet, 1943.

Source B

1 Justice has been trampled under foot. It must be raised again.

2 Freedom of faith and of conscience will be safeguarded.

3 The dignity of the human person must be recognized as the basis for the order of justice and peace.

▲ From a programme produced by the Kreisau Circle (an important Christian group) in 1943.

What would come after Hitler?

It was difficult to see who would rule after Hitler (see Source D). One of the most respected men who spoke out against Hitler was **Dietrich Bonhoeffer**. Many people who were against Hitler thought Bonhoeffer could have led Germany. Bonhoeffer, however, never had the chance to lead Germany – he was executed by the SS in April 1945.

DIETRICH BONHOEFFER (1906–45)

Bonhoeffer had studied theology in Germany and the USA. He was pastor of a German Protestant Church. From 1934 on he spoke against Hitler's policies towards the church and other minority groups.

He tried to plot against Hitler and gain the help of the Allies, but he was arrested by the Gestapo in April 1943. He was sent to Flossenburg concentration camp. He was executed there in 1945. Many people had seen him as the best person to succeed Hitler.

Source C

Germans:
Monstrous things have taken place under our eyes in the years past. Against the advice of all his experts, Hitler has sacrificed whole armies for his desire for glory...to maintain his power, he has made a reign of terror...destroying justice...

We must not continue on that course!... Without hatred, we will attempt to bring Germans together again. With dignity, we will attempt peace with other countries.

▲ Adapted from an appeal which General Beck would have made if Hitler had been killed in 1944.

Source D

The main difficulty with Beck is that he is very theoretical, a man of tactics but little willpower, whereas Goerdeler has great willpower but no tactics. I have always feared that we have too little contact with younger circles.

▲ From entries in von Hassell's diary, December 1941.

QUESTIONS

1 Read page 89. Write down the four different groups of people who formed the resistance to Hitler after 1941.

2 Read Sources A and B. What did these two groups want which Hitler had destroyed?

5.6 The end of the Third Reich

The beginnings of defeat

In 1943, the Red Army of the Soviet Union defeated the German army at **Stalingrad**. This was a major turning point.

From then on the British and Americans began to drive the Germans out of Italy and France. At the same time the Red Army drove the Germans steadily back out of the Soviet Union.

Hitler's attitude to defeat

Hitler refused to think of defeat. He blamed everyone else for what had happened. He blamed the German people for being soft. He blamed the other German leaders. He blamed the army. And finally, of course, he blamed the Jews.

The final defeat

In April 1945, the British and Americans were advancing towards Berlin (Germany's capital city) from the west. The Red Army was advancing on Berlin from the east. Hitler took cyanide and shot himself. Goebbels then burnt Hitler's body and shot himself.

Collapse of the Third Reich

Hitler had called his great German state the Third Reich. It collapsed within a week of his death and Germany came under the control of the Allies who had won the war.

Discovery of the concentration camps

The soldiers of the Soviet Union, Britain and the USA discovered the concentration camps. They were horrified by what they found.

Justice

The Allies wanted to bring the Nazi leaders to justice. They started to search for them. Some, however, were already dead. Hitler, Goebbels and Bormann had killed themselves. Himmler took cyanide.

Source A

Wars are decided by one side recognizing that they cannot win. We must show the enemy that they can never reckon on our surrender. Never!

▲ Hitler speaking in April 1945.

Source B

I have no successor. Hess is insane. Goering has lost the sympathy of the nation.

▲ Hitler's Will and Testament, April 1945.

Source C

It is untrue that I or anybody else in Germany wanted war in 1939. It was wanted by international statesmen who were Jewish or with Jewish interests.

▲ From Hitler's Will and Testament, April 1945.

Source D

◄ The Nuremberg Trials 1946.

Source E

It is my wish to be burned in the place where I worked during my twelve years' service to my people.

▲ Hitler speaking in April 1945.

The Nuremberg Trials 1946

The other Nazi leaders including Goering, Hess and Streicher were put on trial in 1946 at Nuremberg. They were charged with war crimes and crimes against humanity. Most of them said they had been obeying orders. Some were put in prison and some were hanged. Some were allowed to go free.

QUESTIONS

1 Read page 91.

   a Why was the Battle of Stalingrad a turning point in the war?
   b Who did Hitler blame for Germany's defeat?

2 Why did the Allies hold their Nuremberg Trials?

SUMMARY

▶ **1939–41** *Blitzkrieg.*

▶ **1939** Invasion of Poland.

▶ **1940** Conquest of Denmark, Norway, Netherlands, Belgium, France.

▶ **1941** Invasion of the USSR.

▶ **1941–5** Total war.

▶ **1942** Turning points in the War: the Battles of Stalingrad and El Alamein.

▶ **1943–4** Heaviest Allied bombing of Germany.

▶ **1945** Allied discovery of the concentration and extermination camps.

▶ **1945** (April/May) Hitler's suicide and surrender of Germany.

▶ **1946** Nuremberg Trials.

Source 1

A certain air of modest prosperity pervaded the streets . . . Most were ready to admit that there was quite a lot to be said for the New Order . . . Look at young Heini, for instance, with his neatly clipped pate, so purposeful, so different from the long-haired lout who propped up the street corner some months back, and Father . . . with his [Nazi] Party badge.

▲ Christabel Bielenberg, a young English woman married to a German lawyer, gives her impressions of how ordinary Germans viewed their country under the Nazi régime during the mid-1930s.

Source 2

Though the outbreak of war was not greeted with popular enthusiasm, the extraordinary victories of 1939–42 were. The Führer seemed possessed of superhuman abilities. As victories changed to defeat, severe losses were experienced on the Russian front, German cities were pounded ceaselessly night and day by British and American planes and strict economic controls were enforced by Speer as he rapidly increased war production. Hitler disappeared from public view.

▲ Modern historian Martin Roberts describing how defeats changed Germany during the course of the Second World War.

Source 3

◀ Bomb victims in Mannheim, 1944. By the end of the War many people lived in ruined buildings.

▶ A German eyewitness account of Hamburg on the morning after a heavy bombing raid.

Source 4

Weds morning, 28 July 1943
There was no gas, no electricity, not a drop of water, neither the lift nor the telephone was working. It is hard to imagine the panic and chaos. There were no trams, no Underground, no rail-traffic to the suburbs. Most people loaded some belongings on carts, bicycles, prams, or carried things on their backs, and started on foot, just to get away, to escape. People who were wearing [Nazi] party badges had them torn off their coats and there were screams of 'Let's get that murderer'. The police did nothing.

1 a According to Source 1 what was the attitude of the German people to the Nazis in the mid-1930s?

   b Read Source 4. Had the attitude of the German people changed by 1943?

2 What do sources 2, 3 and 4 tell you about the effect of the War on German civilians?

3 Why would Hitler have 'disappeared from public view' (Source 2) as soon as the bombing of German cities started and defeat looked likely?

GLOSSARY

anti-Semitism a phrase used to describe hatred of Jewish people; first used in the late 19th century.

autobahn a 'superhighway' consisting of four lanes. Hitler carried out a programme of highway construction which, at its height, employed 70,000 people.

Bolsheviks a group, led by Lenin, which overthrew the Provisional Government in October 1917, and turned Russia into a communist country.

capitalism an economic system where industries and businesses are in the hands of private individuals. Powerful capitalists in Nazi Germany included Gustav Krupp and Fritz Thyssen who both owned large steelworks and supported Hitler.

degenerate art the name given by Hitler to forms of modern art which he disliked. Hitler confiscated over 12,000 paintings which he said were degenerate. Hitler approved of paintings which showed scenes such as Nazis marching.

demilitarize to keep free of soliders and military installations. Under the Treaty of Versailles no German troops were allowed in the Rhineland (the part of Germany which directly bordered France).

democracy system whereby the whole population in theory has a say in the government through elected representatives. A democratic society is tolerant and classless.

Kreisau Circle a group of about twenty army officers and middle-class civilians set up in 1933 to oppose Hitler. They believed that the Nazis spelt disaster for Germany.

putsch an attempt to seize power using violence.

reparations payments made by Germany to the victorious nations after the First World War to compensate for the damage done.

republic a country where there is no monarchy and the head of state is called a president.

Ruhr the most important coal mining and steel-making area in Germany. French troops invaded Ruhr in January 1923 after the German government said it was unable to pay reparations.

Third Reich the word 'Reich' means 'empire'. The First Reich lasted from 962 until 1806. The Second Reich was set up by Otto von Bismarck in 1871. It lasted until 1918, when it was replaced by the Weimar Republic. The Third Reich was the Nazi régime of Hitler, which lasted from 1933–45.

totalitarian state a country where the government controls all aspects of life. There are no free elections. Secret police and censorship are used as instruments of control. Only one political party is permitted.

Wall Street Crash the collapse of the American Stock Exchange, situated in Wall Street, New York, on 29 October 1929. The crash heralded the start of the Great Depression of the 1930s.

INDEX